Jessica Fischer, Gesa Stedman (eds.)
Imagined Economies – Real Fictions

Culture & Theory | Volume 210

Jessica Fischer is a lecturer and researcher in Literary and Cultural Studies. She studied English, History of Art, European Cultural Studies, and Cultural and Social Anthropology at the University of Freiburg, the Freie Universität Berlin, and the University College London. At Humboldt-Universität zu Berlin, she wrote her doctoral thesis entitled *Agency. The Entrepreneurial Self in Narratives of Transformation*. Her research involves Cultural Studies, Postcolonial Studies, Postclassical Narratology, Social Philosophy and Anthropology.

Gesa Stedman is professor of British culture and literature and the Director of the Centre for British Studies at the Humboldt-Universität zu Berlin. She has edited a large number of special issues, e.g. for *The Journal of the Study of British Cultures*, as well as edited collections, most recently on Brexit and the Arts.

JESSICA FISCHER, GESA STEDMAN (EDS.)

Imagined Economies – Real Fictions

New Perspectives on Economic Thinking in Great Britain

[transcript]

The publication of this work was supported by the Open Access Publication Fund of Humboldt-Universität zu Berlin.

Bibliographic information published by the Deutsche Nationalbibliothek
The Deutsche Nationalbibliothek lists this publication in the Deutsche Nationalbibliografie; detailed bibliographic data are available in the Internet at http://dnb.d-nb.de

First published in 2020 by transcript Verlag, Bielefeld
© Jessica Fischer, Gesa Stedman (eds.)

Cover layout: Kordula Röckenhaus, Bielefeld
Cover illustration: Janina Fischer, »Bubble Man«
Proofread by Corinna Radke, Catherine Smith and David Bell
Typeset by Corinna Radke

Print-ISBN 978-3-8376-4881-2
PDF-ISBN 978-3-8394-4881-6
https://doi.org/10.14361/9783839448816

Table of Contents

Introduction
Jessica Fischer and Gesa Stedman | 7

Why *Imagined* Economies?
John Clarke | 17

The Rise and Decline of *Doux Commerce*:
Change of Experience and Change of Perception
Christiane Eisenberg | 35

The Emotional Economies of Colonial Capitalism
and Its Legacies
Jana Gohrisch | 55

Imagining Money
Jason G. Allen | 79

Beneath and Beyond the City:
The Multiple Faces of British Finance
Olivier Butzbach | 101

A Nation of Shopkeepers?
The Idealised High Street in Brexit Britain
Rebecca Bramall | 119

The New Democratic Economy:
An Imaginary and Real Alternative
Luke Martell | 139

Imaginary Economies:
Narratives for the 21st Century
Melissa Kennedy | 157

Authors | 175

Introduction[1]

Jessica Fischer and Gesa Stedman

Who would have thought it? Neoliberalism has survived the economic crisis of 2007-2008 although it has proved to be illogical, dysfunctional and dangerous (Harvey). "Nothing substantial has been altered in the infrastructure of the global financial system from its state before the crisis. [...] Neoliberalism is alive and well" (Mirowski 8, 28). Or, as Ngai-Ling Sum and Bob Jessop attest, "the neoliberal imaginary remains dominant and continues to shape imagined economic recoveries" (Sum and Jessop 428). Apparently unquestioned, solutions for the disaster are based on the structural causes of the disaster. Trying to make sense of this situation, numerous publications are dedicated to the post-crisis circumstances, with fitting titles such as *The Strange Non-Death of Neoliberalism* (Crouch). It is strange indeed: neoliberal models continue to play a major role in public policies of the 21st century. Great Britain, for instance, suffered severely from the consequences of the financial crash. The Conservative and Liberal Democrat coalition government introduced the United Kingdom government austerity programme in 2010, thereby making the average citizen responsible for the failures of the financial system. Instead of rethinking a political agenda once set by

---

1   This introduction derives in part from Jessica Fischer, Agency. The Entrepreneurial Self in Narratives of Transformation: Debuting in the Literary Field at the Dawn of the Twenty-First Century. Publisher tba, forthcoming.

Margaret Thatcher, and continued in slightly changed shape under Tony Blair, former Prime Minister David Cameron's vision of a Big Society with a small welfare state extended neoliberal reforms. Instead of pinpointing structural conditions which led to the financial crisis, he strengthened the focus on the individual subject. Unimaginable?

In fact, it is its imaginability that allows neoliberal capitalism to stay alive after the crash. In *Das Gespenst des Kapitals* (2010), Joseph Vogl analyses the (in)coherence of economic models as well as the inconsistent interpretations of irregular events in finance business. He also highlights the unreadability of the markets. Most importantly, he brings to the fore the discrepancy between economic theories and economic realities. Theoretically, rational agents compete on decentralised markets undisturbed by chaotic coincidences. In our realities, neither entirely decentralised markets nor a balanced distribution of economic resources by rational agents exist. Thus, economic theorists deal with a powerful imaginary. They keep alive a liberal "Oikodizee" by *projecting* a reality (Vogl 54, 55). "This forms the double structure of modern economic thought or [...] its performative power: Its concept of the market is both model and veridiction and hence connected with the imperative to make the laws of the market real yourself" (55).[2] Subjects are compelled to enact an idea which is framed as 'truth'. By enacting the idea, they make it real and, hence, true. If the realisation fails, it is the individual's failure to perform truth. So, a vital part of (imagined) economies are certain types of subjects that are willing to perform these imaginaries.

Michel Foucault, Ulrich Bröckling and Marnie Holborow, for example, have identified the *homo economicus* as key to the reproduction of contemporary economies. Economist Michael Hutter and legal scholar

---

2   Translation by Jessica Fischer. The original text says: "Das prägt die doppelte Struktur des modernen ökonomischen Wissens oder [...] seine performative Kraft: Das Konzept des Markts ist darin Modell und Wahrheitsprogramm zugleich und also mit der Aufforderung verbunden, Marktgesetze selbst wahr zu machen."

Gunther Teubner termed the *homo economicus* a "Realfiktion" (Hutter and Teubner), both a fiction and a reality. This real fiction shapes our everyday discourses and practices, aids neoliberalism and makes subjectification to it natural or common-sense in a Gramscian logic. This real fiction is a way to "conduct the conduct of men" (Foucault 186). Addressed as *homo economicus*, we accept the market as a site of veridiction and are inclined to commodify every aspect of our life. By making us economic men, a particular regime of truth (in the Foucauldian sense) allows neoliberalism to become real. Moreover, neoliberalism is able to become real because we *want* to turn ourselves into economic men. The expectations by society intersect with the desire of the individual. We want to be entrepreneurial – and we should be. Nevertheless, the real fiction of the *homo economicus* is but one facet of a wider imaginary. Many more facets can be traced. "The Economy now commands the stage, such that [...] other domains [such as politics, culture, sociality, the state] appear subordinate or even subservient to the Economy and its needs," claims John Clarke in his chapter (Clarke 18). Thus, it is necessary to keep investigating our everyday discourses and practices in order to question the assumed hegemony[3] of the Economy. It is particularly necessary for the investigation to think of economies as imagined. "The idea of imagined economies opens the space for a certain type of critical engagement with contemporary political economy," promises Clarke (95). The idea of economies as real fictions invites a less obvious approach and more variety, an analysis against the grain.

A look back into the history of economic thought and historical models of the economy shows how heavily intertwined the imagination and the economy – both in thought and act – have always been. It is remarkable how the presentism of the neoliberal age has managed to make us forget the historicity of the economy, and hence the possibility of imagining it otherwise, and of enacting it otherwise. In her recently published book *Kapitalismus, Märkte und Moral* (2019), the historian Ute Frevert

---

3   It is important to note that we follow Antonio Gramsci's idea that hegemony is never static or completed (Gramsci).

explores early examples of the criticism directed at what we now call capitalism. She points out that its early reformers argued on a moral basis and thus forced capitalism in its then current form to adapt and that it is this moral criticism, even outrage, based as it is on imagining things otherwise, which forces historical change up to this day. Whether that was always the case must remain for the historians to decide. We would argue that it is necessary not only to imagine the economy differently, but to actually enact it differently, since capitalism is adept at incorporating elements of criticism, e.g. ecological concerns, by turning them into consumerism but without ever changing the fundamental opposition between the many and the few.

How to make alternatives to the current economic model, e.g. an economy which incorporates the concept of a guaranteed basic income (Bauman), become real fictions, rather than outlandish minority positions, is a question addressed by some of the contributions to this volume. They do so by re-writing the history of economic thought and reminding us that, at least in the British case, this history rests on racist exploitation, forgotten in most of today's accounts (cf. Gohrisch in this volume) or morphed into nostalgic pseudo-histories which, rather than being true explorations and analyses of the past, serve contemporary needs for nostalgia (cf. Bramall in this volume; Bauman). Luke Martell tackles alternative models of economic thought and action with his analysis of the Labour Party's positions and their application in Preston in the North of England, where an attempt has been made to set up a community-based circular economy to keep profit in the community, rather than letting it go to transnational conglomerate bodies. That this kind of action can be harnessed both by right-wing and left-wing political groups is down less to the actual workings of the model, but rather to the attached imagined communities to which it appeals. Does wealth in the community necessarily entail a parochial, nationalist or even regionalist worldview and political agenda? Who defines who belongs to such a community? How can one avoid social and political exclusion on the one hand and transnational profiteering on the other?

Rebecca Bramall's chapter explores a related issue, namely, the nostalgic, constructed character of The High Street and how it is represented, invoked and used for contemporary political and economic arguments. She shows that "(t)he idealised high street sustains both reactionary and radical visions of national identity and of the role of the economy in a future society. Both have a nostalgic dimension, and so it is vital to scrutinise the ways in which nostalgia for former modes of economic organisation can naturalise exclusions on the basis of race or class." (Bramall 134). The high street can be mobilised both for reactionary causes or for the Labour Party's new policies and similar progressive political projects. Jana Gohrisch throws a light on how current ethnic exclusion mechanisms and institutional racism in Britain rest on the way in which the management of anger has allowed the majority society to conveniently forget that its position of power rests on the exploitation of slave workers in the past. By reading recent anti-racist publications by prominent Black writers such as Reno Eddo-Lodge or Afua Hirsch in conjunction with the 19th-century novel *Lutchmee and Dilloo. A Study of West Indian Life* by Edward Jenkins (1877), she is able to show how "emotions always key into the economy – imagined and real" (Gohrisch 74).

Melissa Kennedy also makes a case for the importance of fictional narratives or literary and cultural studies in relation to economics. With Aesop's fable "The Ant and the Grasshopper" as an example, she explains economics as a "narrative of human interaction, invented and imagined into being" (Kennedy 158) and assigns to literary criticism the ability to discuss these narratives in new ways. Framing economics as social science and 'the economy' not in the narrow meaning of finance and market but in the broader sense of human economies further connects economics to literary studies: both disciplines shape, analyse and critique the "symbolic, cultural, social, and political expressions of human exchange and interaction" (Kennedy 160). Drawing this connection between economics and fictional narratives or literary/cultural studies also encourages alternative imaginaries to hegemonic discourses about 'the economy'. Several popular economics texts published after the financial crisis, for instance, tap into literary/cultural imagery in order to question dominant ideas about what the economy is and how the economy works. These texts propose a rethinking of human interaction under the heading 'economy'. This, moreover, "offers a reinvigorated role for the humanities, particularly literary studies" (Kennedy 164).

Christiane Eisenberg takes a historical view on a rethinking of human exchange. In her chapter about the rise and decline of *doux commerce*, she investigates the changing perception of this figure of thought from the late 17th and 18th centuries and the changing experience to which it led. In France and Germany, the term 'commerce' mostly meant "sociability, communication and social intercourse (also between the sexes)" whereas the British "also included the economic relations between market participants" (Eisenberg 35). *Doux commerce* according to the British definition premised activities such as trading, buying or selling as a way of bringing subjects peacefully together even if they had opposing interests. These activities were hoped to increase mutual trust and eventually decrease unequal power relations. In other words: by generalising commerce "society as a whole would benefit" (Eisenberg 36). For her diachronic approach to *doux commerce*, Christiane Eisenberg takes into account the history of markets and the market economy in Britain as well as the changing social and political power relations with which they were entangled. Her aim is to raise an awareness for the complexity of equalling market society and civil society.

Olivier Butzbach historicises another real fiction of British economy – that of 'the City', London's financial district. In his chapter, he acknowledges the status of the City as one of the "most entrenched visions of modern capitalism" (Butzbach 101) and explores its contradictions. The City seems to be both the embodiment of the markets and a representation of concentrated power. Butzbach investigates the City as a problematic example of some misleading connotations it has evoked. He also analyses the performative power which it has nevertheless gained in the past. A simplified conception of the British financial system as a system of markets or as a small but strong network of financial institutions in London had far-reaching political consequences. It influenced Thatcherite and New Labour policy-makers with regard to financial regulation. In both cases the City had to be upheld as a centre of global finance and as an autonomous space with unchained financial markets – which was assumed to be a guarantee for continuous economic growth. "The disastrous outcomes of such approaches, revealed by the 2007-08 financial crisis, thus show how necessary it is to rethink the place and role of the City in British finance" (Butzbach 104). Hence, Butzbach argues for a more nuanced characterisation of British finance and of economies in both their material as well as symbolic aspects.

Jason Allen's chapter looks at a fundamental element of the economy, at least in its Western incarnation: money. Difficult to define, with multiple functions and shapes, lawyers try to circumscribe the functions and use of money. With the advent of virtual forms of money, as well as high finance, the always rather tenuous relationship between money and its material base has become even more flimsy. This historical shift also argues for a shift in imagination: "Perhaps the crucial virtue in anyone thinking about the future of money at the present time would be imagination – the courage to take a moment, to reject the inevitability of legacy conventions, and to imagine what might be possible in the future" (Allen 96). Allen's statement about the future of money also applies to 'the economy' in general. Future possibilities are imagined and communicated, for instance by Thomas Piketty in his new book on capitalism and ideology (Piketty)[4]. Next to contextualising our current economic system and its conceptual underpinnings, Piketty promises a new model which is meant to overcome social inequalities.

This edited collection developed from the lecture series 'Imagined Economies' which took place at the Centre for British Studies, Humboldt-Universität zu Berlin, in 2018. We are aware that imagined economies are "discursively constituted and materially reproduced on many sites and scales, in different spatio-temporal contexts, and over various

---

4   The English translation of Piketty's publication is available from March 2020.

spatio-temporal horizons" (Sum and Jessop 174), that there is an endless array of research fields and potential questions we could follow. With *Imagined Economies – Real Fictions. New Perspectives on Economic Thinking in Great Britain* our authors identify *some* of the sites and scales of (Britain's) imagined economies. The aim is to connect seemingly separate fields such as finance and fiction in order to better understand current political changes in Great Britain and beyond. In addition, this publication offers an urgently needed interdisciplinary view of the performative power of economic thought. It opens a space not only for a critical engagement with 'economies' but also for fresh imaginations.

We owe a debt of gratitude to all authors who shared first ideas and final articles about imagined economies. A special thank-you goes to Corinna Radke, Catherine Smith and David Bell for proofreading and copy-editing our manuscripts. We could not have completed our publication without them or the staff of transcript Verlag. Further, we want to thank photographer Janina Fischer for the cover image. Many thanks to those who helped to make this collection become 'real'. We are also grateful to our colleagues and students at the Centre for British Studies of Humboldt-Universität zu Berlin who stimulate interdisciplinary research and constantly foster the development of new ideas for lecture series, projects, and books.

REFERENCES

Bauman, Zygmunt. *Retrotopia*. Polity Press, 2017.

Bröckling, Ulrich. *Das unternehmerische Selbst. Soziologie einer Subjektivierungsform*. 5th ed., Suhrkamp, 2013.

Clarke, John. "Imagined, Real and Moral Economies." *Culture Unbound: Journal of Current Cultural Research,* vol. 6, 2014, pp. 95-112.

Crouch, Colin. *The Strange Non-Death of Neoliberalism*. Polity Press, 2011.

Fischer, Jessica. *Agency. The Entrepreneurial Self in Narratives of Transformation: Debuting in the Literary Field at the Dawn of the Twenty-First Century.* Publisher tba, forthcoming.

Foucault, Michel. *The Birth of Biopolitics. Lectures at the Collège de France, 1978-1979.* Edited by Michel Senellart, translated by Graham Burchell, Palgrave Macmillan, 2008.

Frevert, Ute. *Kapitalismus, Märkte und Moral.* Residenz Verlag, 2019.

Gramsci, Antonio. *Selections from Prison Notebooks.* Translated and edited by Quintin Hoare and Geoffrey Nowell-Smith, Lawrence and Wishart, 1971.

Harvey, David. *A Brief History of Neoliberalism.* Oxford University Press, 2005.

Holborow, Marnie. *Language and Neoliberalism.* Routledge, 2015.

Hutter, Michael, and Gunther Teubner. "Der Gesellschaft fette Beute. Homo juridicus und homo oeconomicus als kommunikationserhaltende Fiktionen." *Der Mensch – das Medium der Gesellschaft*, edited by Peter Fuchs and Andreas Göbel, Suhrkamp, 1994, pp. 110-45.

Mirowski, Philip. *Never Let a Serious Crisis Go to Waste. How Neoliberalism Survived the Financial Meltdown.* Verso, 2013.

Piketty, Thomas. *Capital et idéologie.* Le Seuil, 2019.

Sum, Ngai-Ling and Bob Jessop. *Towards A Cultural Political Economy. Putting Culture in its Place in Political Economy.* Edward Elgar, 2014.

Vogl, Joseph. *Das Gespenst des Kapitals.* Diaphenes, 2010.

Why *Imagined* Economies?

John Clarke

I begin with a puzzle: why talk about *imagined* economies? In everyday
life, economies appear to be exactly the opposite of 'imagined': they are
material, substantial, overpowering, forceful and constantly demanding
our attention. Indeed, we are immersed in economies: we inhabit a
global economy, a regional economy, a national economy (and live with
the unsettling intersection between them). More abstractly, there are dis-
cussions about financial economies (and their opposite 'real economies'); the learning economy and the knowledge economy are offered
as new formations; some talk about the relationships between the Global
North and South in terms of neo-colonial economies. In other settings,
including academic ones, people have talked and written of political
economies, moral economies and social economies, while more recently, I have encountered ideas of cultural economies, affective econo-
mies and domestic economies. This feels like a lot of economies and one
of the things that adding the word 'imagined' does for me is to interrupt
the apparent ubiquity of economies: it creates what might be called 'a
pause for thought'. Such a pause for thought is potentially productive
given the ubiquity and omnipotence of the economy and all these economies.

Thinking about imagined economies creates the possibility of questioning both the proliferation of economies and the assumed potency of
the Economy (in the singular). From being one social domain among

many (politics, culture, sociality, the state, etc.), the Economy now commands the stage, such that those other domains now appear subordinate or even subservient to the Economy and its needs. For many this is associated with the rise of neoliberalism as a political and ideological project that includes what Harvey calls the 'commodification of everything' (Harvey 165). The dominance of the Economy (and its shadow self – logics of economic calculation) has transformed social, political and cultural domains, subjecting them to the rule of the market, either in the direct form of 'market forces', or through the creation of quasi-markets (forms of regulation that aim to mimic the dynamics of 'real' markets via mechanisms of competition and contracting [Le Grand]). I will come back to markets later, but for now, they form part of the sheer cultural weight of the Economy in its singular forcefulness: the proclaimed absence of any alternative to the logic of the economy's need to grow and be unbounded, especially its need to be liberated from state regulation or political interference. This logic of 'economic realism' – summed up in Margaret Thatcher's famous phrase 'There Is No Alternative' (TINA) – has dominated debates about social reform, public spending and the role of the state on a global scale (both in terms of its spread across countries and its domination of global institutions such as the International Monetary Fund, the World Bank and the World Trade Organization).

For a brief period, the global financial crisis of 2007-8 threatened to unlock this economic realist logic, but by 2010 the various rescue missions (designed to save capitalism from itself) had restored the conditions for 'business as usual' and much of the world became subject to a new form of economic realism – Austerity politics and policies (see, *inter alia*, Evans and McBride; Forkert). Austerity announced the economic necessity (in the form of public debt) for reductions in public spending, the greater privatisation of the public realm and the reform of welfare provisions. The needs of the Economy had to be put first. This voracious and needy Economy circulates in the form of representations: images, ideas, moral tales, official reports, statistical indices, graphs and charts and the ubiquitous stock exchange data (addressing us as members of a 'share owning society'). These representations both demand our attention (as the basic stuff of life) and simultaneously demand our critical attention. As David Ruccio has argued:

> The fact is, there are diverse representations of the economy – what it is, how it operates, how it is intertwined with the rest of the natural and social world, what concepts are appropriate to analyzing it, and so on – in all three arenas: within the official discipline of economics, in academic departments and research centers other than departments of economics within colleges and universities, and in activities and institutions outside the academy. And the diversity of economic representations that exists in these arenas simply cannot be reduced to or captured by a singular definition, including the all-too-common statements about 'how economists think' or what the 'central economic question is' that one finds in the textbooks that are used every year, around the world, to teach hundreds of thousands of students how to think about the economy – in other words, how to represent the economy, to themselves and others. (895-6)

As a result, I suggest that there is social and political value in taking a step back from the ever-present demands of His Majesty the Economy and opening up a small space for thought by inserting the word 'imagined' into our thinking about economies. This conceptual move has become increasingly visible across the social sciences, even if both the object being 'imagined' and the practices of imagining are rather different. For example, writers as different as Cornelius Castoriadis and Charles Taylor have explored 'social imaginaries', while writers like Davina Cooper have explored how imagining might function as a social and political practice. Benedict Anderson famously deconstructed nations as 'imagined communities' and states have been examined as imagined formations following Abrams' formative exploration of the 'state idea' (see, for example, Blom Hansen and Stepputat; Cooper et al., *Reimagining the State*; Mitchell; Painter). Finally, some scholars have begun the exploration of imagined economies (Cameron and Palan, in relation to globalisation; see also Clarke, "Imagined, Real"). For me, one critical point of orientation has always been Louis Althusser's thesis that "[i]deology represents the imaginary relationship of individuals to their real conditions of existence" (162). How else do we understand our conditions of existence (economic and more) except through *imaginary* relationships? It is true that a whole set of problems flow from Althusser's proposition – about the character of ideology, the nature of the real conditions and more, but those are for another time. Here, I want to underline both the diversity and productivity of approaches to the imagined and imaginary quality of social phenomena. The singular Economy has a number of richly imagined elements – it is productive (and centred on the labour of production); it is embodied in private property (as wealth, capital or simply the skills that the individual can bring to bear in the market); it is driven by the promise of endless growth and it relies (in theory) on the market to solve the problems of distribution (everything and everyone achieves their value in the market place). In the following sections, I consider the imagined nature of the market that has been central to the processes of economic realism and neo-liberalisation. In the final section, I return to some of these issues (production, private property, the promise of growth and the politics of distribution) to explore the possibility of thinking economies otherwise.

MAKING UP MARKETS

The drive to open up the world to markets involved imagining economies in particular ways, centred on a contrast between the shackled 'managed economies' of post-war Fordism (driven into decline by excessive state interference) and the liberated dynamics of a 'free market', understood as the 'natural' state of the economy. Rescuing the market from its oppressors would, we were promised, ensure freedom (of choice) and entrepreneurialism, uniting producers and consumers in a dynamic of expansive growth. Thomas Frank has written about the compelling rise of market imagery and the way it envisages the market as being able to meet all human needs, articulated by 'market populists' who were

> adherents of a powerful new political mythology that had arisen from the ruins of the thirty-year backlash. Their fundamental faith was a simple one. The market and the people – both understood as grand principles of social life rather than particulars – were essentially one and the same. By its very nature the market was democratic, perfectly expressing the popular will through the machinery of supply and demand, poll and focus group, super-store and Internet. In fact, the market was more democratic than any of the formal institutions of democracy – elections, legislatures, government. The market was a community. The market was infinitely diverse, permitting without prejudice the articulation of any and all tastes and preferences. Most importantly of all, the market was militant about its democracy. It had no place for snobs, for hierarchies, for elitism, for pretense, and it would fight these things by its very nature. (29)

The market, in these imaginaries, was endlessly dynamic, driving eco-nomic, social and political change as people were themselves liberated from their state of dependency (on the state). One critical element of this re-imagining of the relationships between markets, states and societies was provided by public choice theory, which offered a market-centric critique of public service 'monopolies' (Niskanen). Public choice theory demonstrated that, without the discipline of market dynamics (competi-tion) public monopolies would be sclerotic and inefficient, serving the vested interests of producers (see, for example, Friedman and Fried-man's critique of the 'tyranny of the status quo'). Across economic text books, policy programmes and political discourse, the markets that pop-ulated this imagined economy were startlingly similar, resembling noth-ing so much as a projection of how markets might work if abstracted from any social and economic conditions. These abstracted markets were abstracted from the material effects of time and space – as if ex-changes took place instantaneously (and between perfectly informed transactors). Even if particular markets showed evidence of failure (the housing market or the internal market introduced into UK health services, for example), their conditions of failure were always particular. The Stanford professor (and Kaiser Permanente healthcare corporation advisor) Alain Enthoven's relationship to the NHS perfectly captures this tendency. As one of the original advisors on marketising NHS reform he promoted the internal market (*Reflections*); he later returned to review progress and was rather disappointed (*In Pursuit*), suggesting that the initial reforms did not go far enough in marketising health care. This is reminiscent of Jamie Peck's argument that we need to consider the 'turgid reality of neoliberalism variously failing and flailing *forwards*' (7; my emphasis).

This recurrent celebration of the market as the natural and necessary human condition (as against the artificiality and 'social engineering' associated with the state) was a powerful force in normalising the many markets that were created from the mid-1970s onwards. But the naturalising imagery tends to conceal the fact that markets of many different kinds are the result of social and political labour: they have to be made, as Julia Elyachar has argued:

> The notion of the market is so familiar that we tend to take it for granted. But like so many things that we take for granted, we don't really know what it is. "The market" functions as a folk concept more than a scientific term... Rather than the market, we need to think about a multiplicity of markets that are the outcomes of specific forms of labor, culture, technological mixes, and modes of organization specific to time and place. (15, 24)

In particular, it is important to recognise that markets and market-mimicking devices (internal contracting, quasi-markets, etc.) require people to understand themselves as specific sorts of economic agents (motivated and empowered by economic means). Anthropological work on markets, such as Elyachar's, suggests that economic agents are not born, but have to be made. A study of 'citizen-consumers' in England revealed people who were profoundly reluctant to identify themselves as 'consumers of public services', rejecting the impersonal and transactional model that such an identity implied (Clarke et al., *Creating Citizen-Consumers*). Enabling people to think economically, and especially to imagine themselves as economic agents, involves a process of construction that requires intensive political and discursive work (this section draws on Newman and Clarke, chapter 4). For example, the reform of public services through market mechanisms involved the invention of a range of economic agents, each invested with a specific form of power or authority; for instance:

- Provider organisations were invited to imagine themselves as a business, or at least as performing in 'business-like' ways;
- Senior figures in organisations are invited to understand themselves as chief executives, strategic managers or, most recently, leaders. Across the range of public services, this development of senior, strategic, innovative or even transformational management is one of the long-term and now deeply embedded effects of the 'new managerialism'. The proliferation of training and development programmes directed at senior organisational strata encourage two related phenomena: a self-consciousness of being a leader (in the generic sense); and a sense of being the embodiment of the specific corporate entity (providing the vision that motivates others, being the bulwark against external dangers and threats, anticipating the opportunities to 'grow the business').
- Clients, contractors and commissioners were invited to see themselves as purchasers or providers of services. Ideas of how to contract (and manage contracts when established) became part of a new organisational culture, and led to changing relationships (inter-organisational, intra-organisational and inter-personal) that came to be characterised by mutual exploitation, uncertainty and adaptation.
- Workers in organisations were invited to understand themselves as (more or less) valued human resources. In particular, they were expected to imagine themselves as corporate agents – assimilating and executing the organisation's 'mission'. This identification generated

particular sorts of strain in public service organisations, given the historic centrality of bureau-professional roles in which identifications and affiliations tended to be directed as much to the profession as to the specific employing organisation (teachers, social workers, medical staff, etc.). The pressure on organisations to 'think like a business' increased demands for such corporate identification from employees, since professional attachments risked being a distraction from the organisation's conception of its 'core business'.

The *making* of markets involved a process of redrawing boundaries, reconstructing relationships, and inventing new assemblages rather than a simple process of moving from state to market. The process worked through a universalising discourse, albeit one that has not been uniformly successful: people retain attachments to other principles of social life (intimacy, solidarity, publicness, politics) as alternatives to market coordination. People also develop emergent conceptions of alternatives in the face of the failures, costs and consequences of market coordination. Such processes of reform have produced strange new forms of organisation, regulation, coordination and governance, often described as 'hybrids'. Elyachar rightly argues that the process of making markets (or, we might add, market-mimicking processes) is inherently political.

> The labor of making particular forms of markets is also the labor of politics. It is about power. Attempts to teach the poor of Cairo to budget their time and money with more streamlined methods resembling those of capitalist forms, and to learn accounting, "the language of business" [...], are more than ethnographic anomalies. They are attempts to reshape the nature of power and subjectivity. (Elyachar 24)

Elyachar's argument here is important: the work of imagining – making up – markets is not merely abstract invention or the circulation of ideology; rather new forms of power and relationships are brought into being and distributed through such processes. The decentralisation of governmental authority to multiple service providers is one example – highly conditional and delimited authority is devolved by central government to such organisations. Their exercise of it is subject to double pressures: the demands and desires of service users and would-service users on the one side; the apparatuses of inspection and evaluation on the other. Nevertheless, as Pollitt and others have shown, the managers of organisations 'liberated' from direct central or local government control have often relished the 'freedom to manage'. Similarly, citizens as service users are 'empowered' or authorised as consumers to exercise choice over services (in terms of patient or parent choice and in such policy developments as direct payments for social care). But there are also realignments of forms of political and economic power at stake in these processes (or what others have called forms of public and private authority, see Hansen and Salskov-Iversen). These realignments sometimes involve transfers of power and resources (from the state to corporate bodies); they sometimes involve creating fusions or hybrid forms of power (trusts, public private partnerships, social enterprise).

Finally, it might be worth noting an odd disjuncture that occurred in the ways in which markets have been represented in public discourse. The drive to make up markets stressed their dynamism, their efficacy and their energy – markets were transformative institutions. However, by 2008-9 it seemed that markets were not what they used to be. They had become a shadow of their former virile selves, no longer relentlessly expanding but slipping into a period of decline, decay and, above all, depression. Depression is an intriguing term in relation to markets because it condenses two rather different, but significant, clusters of meanings. On the one hand, we encounter the hard evidentiary science of economics – in which depression refers to a specified trend in economic activity, measurable by a set of particular (if contested) indicators. Depressions – like the Great Depression of the 1930s – are profound and prolonged slumps in economic activity. On the other hand, depression is also a key word for describing mental states, emotional moods and clinical psychological conditions. The exchange between these two sites of depression – the economic and the emotional – is intriguing. And there is something fascinating about the proliferation of terms that usually describe mental states and emotional moods to talk about the state of markets. After the 2008-9 crisis, we have become accustomed to hearing about markets that are anxious, nervous, and unsettled. They are, it seems, prone to bouts of panic and hysteria in which they are infected by collective mood swings and a sort of viral irrationality. These mood swings of markets – moments of manic recovery offset by plummeting spirits – threaten to lead us all into depression. And they undermine the claims about dynamism, rationality and the transcendent power of markets.

IMAGINING OTHERWISE

However, the purpose of talking about imagined economies is not just to engage in a challenge to the current dominant imaginaries (a sort of ideology critique). As important is creating the political cultural space for imagining other economies, or even for imagining economies otherwise. In this section I explore some other possible ways of imagining economies: working through different framing devices – economy as reproduction rather than production; economy as commons rather than private property; the possibility of post-growth economies rather than endless growth; and the economy as the focus for a politics of distribution rather than market valuation. I do not claim any great originality about my selection of these issues or my comments on them – but they offer significant contending imaginaries.

How different might economies look if we start from the question of *reproduction* rather than *production*? By this I do not mean the simple model offered in Volume One of Marx's *Capital* of the reproduction of the social relations of production and their embodiments – capital and labour, but an understanding that social reproduction is necessarily expanded and expansive (it is a dynamic process). It is necessarily complex – requiring the reproduction of *all* social relations – and it is also contested. *Contested* reproduction implies that both the content of what is reproduced and the means by which it is reproduced are, in principle, always open to contestation. Being open to contestation does not mean that everything is always and continually in flux. Rather, conflicts arise around particular axes of reproduction in specific sites and become resolved – temporarily – into forms of settlement, resembling what Gramsci described as the 'life of the state': a 'series of unstable equilibria'. The existence of heterogeneous social relations within concrete societies further implies that we have to think about diverse social forces – and their potential for political mobilisation – instead of making the assumption that the only social forces that matter are class forces. The history of social reproduction reveals a range of struggles – from the efforts of organised labour to win 'free time' or protections against market dynamics and market failure, through the struggles of women's organisations over the conditions, costs and consequences of child bearing, to the citizenship rights of groups who have been historically excluded, marginalised and subordinated – such rights being one of the collective conditions of social reproduction. In short, the field of the social (that which has to be reproduced) is itself both complex and contested. Such a starting point would make more visible than usual the work that has to be done to ensure this reproduction – and what happens when that care fails to take place. Brigitte Aulenbacher has argued that from this starting point we might understand care as the fundamental social practice: that without care, nothing – neither people nor the environment – can be adequately reproduced and both suffer profoundly from the *carelessness* of capitalism (Aulenbacher; Aulenbacher et al.).

This understanding of social and material relations as the focal points of economies provides a link to the second imaginary – the idea of the commons. Commoning refers to real practices of governing natural resources for collective use and a political imaginary of how social life might be organised. Peter Linebaugh has argued for the importance of understanding 'the commons' as an active process.

> To speak of the commons as if it were a natural resource is misleading at best and dangerous at worst – the commons is an activity and, if anything, it expresses relationships in society that are inseparable from relations to nature. It might be better to keep the word as a verb, an activity, rather than as a noun, a substantive. (279)

Since Eleanor Ostrom and others challenged Hardin's 1968 description of the 'tragedy of the commons' (the view that common resources were inevitably undermined by the pursuit of economic self-interest), interest in commoning has grown. It has combined investigation of existing practices of commoning, the articulation of policies and procedures for 'governing the commons' and the development of a politics of commoning as an anti-individualist, anti-capitalist ecological economics. It has also been extended into debates about whether a 'social commons' can be imagined, in which questions of social protection and welfare can be rethought as communal resources and rights (see, *inter alia*, Barbagallo and Federici; Mestrum; F. Williams). Mestrum has suggested that

> [w]hen welfare states or social protection are perceived as commons, after a defining and regulating process, they can contribute to collective and individual welfare, as emerging from collective and participatory action. The commons sustain our common being, our being together, our co-existence. They go beyond individual interests. (6)

Two lines of questioning follow from these imaginaries. The first, which reflects the centrality of environmental questions to both reproduction and commoning, asks whether we can imagine a 'post-growth economy'. What Aulenbacher calls 'careless' capitalism has been built on the presumption of endless growth – the promise that there are always new needs to be discovered, new markets to be created, new resources to be mined (literally and metaphorically) and new sources of labour to be put to work. The global crisis that threatens to engulf us all, and its local instantiations (unbreathable air, rising water levels, deforestation, species extermination and more) point precisely to the unsustainability of that economic imaginary. A range of approaches have been developed as ways of living without growth from Bookchin's post-scarcity anarchism to the Post Growth Institute. Bookchin argued that

> [u]nless we realize that the present market society, structured around the brutally competitive imperative of 'grow or die', is a thoroughly impersonal, self-operating mechanism, we will falsely tend to blame technology as such or population growth as such for environmental [and social] problems. We will ignore their root causes, such as trade for profit, industrial expansion, and the identification of 'progress' with corporate self-interest. In short, we will tend to focus on the symptoms of a grim social pathology rather than on the pathology itself, and our efforts will be directed toward limited goals whose attainment is more cosmetic than curative. (463)

The direction and political-cultural dynamics of a post-growth economy remain contested (see, for example, some of the discussion in the special issue of the journal *ephemera*). But the urgency of the questions that are posed there continues to increase as environmental crises multiply and their implications for population movements become more visible.

The second line of questions intersect forcefully with the first, since they concern the future politics of distribution. Ferguson and Li have recently suggested that we have come to the end of two potent economic imaginaries: in the global north the degradation of waged work, the rise of precarity and the rise of automation have meant the end of the 'proper job' (even as Work is increasingly fetishized as the fundamental human activity). In the global south, the 'myth of development' is no longer sustainable (even as it is recycled in new forms). Neither promise – the proper job or urbanising development – can be fulfilled. Indeed, each promise was, even in its heyday, only ever selectively and partially delivered. In the present though, the question of how people might live and how they might make a living, are increasingly pressing matters, locally, nationally and globally – and they demand new ways of thinking about the social surplus and how to control and distribute it.

I have tried to outline one set of things that come into view if we consider *imagined* economies (others are, of course, imaginable). The necessary starting point for me is the unlocking of the projected *economic realism* that underpins and constantly demands our acquiescence to the contemporary imagined economy (the 'real' economy). Understanding the myths, stories, fantasies and fictions that work to sustain the apparent necessity of the dominant way of 'doing' the economy is a necessary critical moment. But, as Raymond Williams argued, it is important to look beyond the dominant to see the residual and emergent cultural-political forms that intersect and struggle with it. I have said little about the residual, although another essay might have explored ideas of the 'real economy' (in a world of immaterial flows); the nostalgia for 'proper jobs' (and its correlate 'real men', perhaps); the lingering attachment to ideas of social security and social protection (rather than thinly punitive welfare); and the varieties of imagined moral economies, ruled by principles of fairness and 'just deserts', and constrained by the obligations of employers as well as workers. Here, though, I have tried to concentrate on the 'emergent' – economies imagined otherwise around questions of reproduction, care, the commons, the ecological crisis and the politics of distribution. These are not simple fantasies (as economic realists would insist) nor do they form an integrated and coherent political programme. They ask that we think – and act – otherwise. And that is the best possible reason I can find for exploring *imagined* economies.

ACKNOWLEDGEMENTS

I owe a debt of thanks to the organisers for first inviting me to talk about this issue, and then to write about it. I am also grateful to Janet Newman for her comments on an earlier draft. The final section was partly inspired by participation in the Institute for Political Ecology's Green Summer Academy in Vis in 2016 (ipe.hr/en/ipe/about-ipe/).

REFERENCES

Abrams, Philip. "Notes on the Difficulty of Studying the State." 1977. *Journal of Historical Sociology*, vol. 1, no. 1, 1988, pp. 58-89.

Althusser, Louis. "Ideology and Ideological State Apparatuses (Notes towards an Investigation)." *Lenin and Philosophy and Other Essays*, translated by Ben Brewster, Monthly Review Press, 1971, pp. 127-86.

Anderson, Benedict. *Imagined Communities: Reflections on the Origins and Spread of Nationalism*. Verso, 1991.

Aulenbacher, Brigitte. "'It's Care Again.' Care Regimes between Marketization and Charity Economy." Presentation to ZIF Workshop on *Charity Economy: International Dimensions and Political Perspectives*, Bielefeld, 21-23 September 2016.

—, Helma Lutz, and Birgit Riegraf. "Introduction: Towards a Global Sociology of Care and Care Work." *Current Sociology*, vol. 66, no. 4, 2018, pp. 495-502.

Barbagallo, Camille, and Silvia Federici. "Introduction: Care Work and the Commons." *The Commoner*, vol. 15, 2012, pp. 1-21, www.commoner.org.uk/wp-content/uploads/2012/01/commoner_issue-15.pdf.

Bartlett, Will, Jennifer Roberts, and Julian Le Grand. *A Revolution in Social Policy: Quasi-Market Reforms in the 1990s*. The Policy Press, 1998.

Blom Hansen, Thomas, and Finn Stepputat, editors. *States of Imagination: Ethnographic Explorations of the Postcolonial State*. Duke University Press, 2001.

Bookchin, Murray. "What is Social Ecology?" *Environmental Philosophy: From Animal Rights to Radical Ecology*, edited by Michael E. Zimmerman, Prentice Hall, 2005/1993.

Cameron, Angus, and Ronen Palan. *The Imagined Economies of Globalization*. Sage Publications, 2004.

Castoriadis, Cornelius. *The Imaginary Institution of Society*. 1987. Translated by Kathleen Blamey, MIT Press, 1998.

Clarke, John. "Imagined, Real and Moral Economies." *Culture Unbound*, vol. 6, 2014, pp. 95-112, www.cultureunbound.ep.liu.se/article.asp?DOI=10.3384/cu.2000.1525.14695.

—, Janet Newman, Nick Smith, Elizabeth Vidler, and Louise Westmarland. *Creating Citizen-Consumers: Changing Publics and Changing Public Services*. Sage Publications, 2007.

Cooper, Davina. *Everyday Utopias: The Conceptual Life of Promising Spaces*. Duke University Press, 2013.

—, Nikita Dhawan, and Janet Newman, editors. *Reimagining the State*. Routledge, 2019.

Elyachar, Julia. *Markets of Dispossession: NGOs, Economic Development, and the State in Cairo*. Duke University Press, 2005.

Enthoven, Alain. *In Pursuit of an Improving National Health Service*. The Nuffield Trust, 1999.

—. *Reflections on the Management of the NHS*. Nuffield Provincial Hospitals Trust, 1985.

Evans, Bryan, and Stephen McBride, editors. *Austerity: The Lived Experience*. University of Toronto Press, 2017.

Ferguson, James, and Tania Li. *Beyond the "Proper Job": Political-economic Analysis after the Century of Labouring Man*. Working Paper 51, PLAAS, UWC, 2018.

Frank, Thomas. *One Market Under God: Extreme Capitalism, Market Populism and the End of Economic Democracy*. Anchor Books, 2001.

Friedman, Milton, and Rose Friedman. *The Tyranny of the Status Quo*. Harcourt Brace Jovanovich, 1984.

Forkert, Kirsten. *Austerity as Public Mood: Social Anxieties and Social Struggles*. Rowman and Littlefield, 2017.

Garmann Johnsen, Christian, Mette Nelund, Lena Olaison, and Bent Meier Sørensen, editors. "Organizing for the Post-Growth Economy." *Ephemera*, vol. 17, no. 1, February 2017, www.ephemerajournal.org/issue/organizing-post-growth-economy.

Hansen, Hans Krause, and Dorte Salskov-Iversen, editors. *Critical Perspectives on Private Authority in Global Politics*. Palgrave Macmillan, 2007.

Hardin, Garrett. "The Tragedy of the Commons." *Science*, vol. 162, no. 3859, 1968, pp. 1243-48.

Harvey, David. *A Brief History of Neoliberalism*. Oxford University Press, 2005.

Le Grand, Julian. "Quasi-Markets versus State Provision of Public Services; Some Ethical Considerations." *Public Reason*, vol. 3, no. 2, 2011, pp. 80-89.

Linebaugh, Peter. *Magna Carta Manifesto: Liberties and Commons for All*. University of California Press, 2007.

Mestrum, Francine. *Social Commons: a New Alternative to Neoliberalism*. 27 August 2015, eng.globalaffairs.ru/valday/Social-Commons-a-new-alternative-to-neoliberalism-17656.

Mitchell, Timothy. "Society, Economy and the State Effect." *State/Culture: State-Formation after the Cultural Turn*, edited by George Steinmetz, Cornell University Press, 1999, pp. 76-99.

Newman, Janet, and John Clarke. *Publics, Politics and Power: Remaking the Public in Public Services*. Sage Publications, 2009.

Niskanen, William A. *Bureaucracy and Representative Government*. Aldine-Atherton, 1971.

Ostrom, Elinor. *Governing the Commons: The Evolution of Institutions for Collective Action*. Cambridge University Press, 1990.

Painter, Joe. "Prosaic Geographies of Stateness." *Political Geography*, vol. 25, no. 7, 2006, pp. 752-74.

Peck, Jamie. *Constructions of Neo-Liberal Reason*. Oxford University Press, 2010.

Pollitt, Christopher. *Managerialism and the Public Services*. 2nd ed., Basil Blackwell, 1993.

Post Growth Institute. www.postgrowth.org/learn/about-post-growth/.

Ruccio, David F. "Economic Representations: What's at Stake?" *Cultural Studies*, vol. 22, no. 1, 2008, pp. 892-912.

Taylor, Charles. *Modern Social Imaginaries*. Duke University Press, 2004.

Williams. Fiona. "Towards the Welfare Commons: Contestation, Critique and Criticality in Social Policy." *Social Policy Review*, vol. 27, 2015, pp. 93-111.

Williams, Raymond. *Marxism and Literature*. Oxford University Press, 1977.

The Rise and Decline of *Doux Commerce*: Change of Experience and Change of Perception

Christiane Eisenberg

In his book *The Passions and the Interests*, the American economist Albert O. Hirschman reconstructed a figure of thought from the late 17th and 18th centuries based on the idea that a commercial society is a polite, civilised society (Hirschman, *The Passions*; see also Hirschman, "Rival Interpretations"). The key words *commerce* and *doux commerce* fit into an enlightened intellectual discourse on manners and behaviour that had some nationally specific accentuations. While French and German participants were accustomed to using the term *commerce* primarily in the sense of sociability, communication and social intercourse (also between the sexes) the British also included the economic relations between market participants. For thinkers like John Locke, David Hume and Sir James Steuart, to name but a few, this was exactly what made the figure of thought so attractive. This special accentuation was also noted by foreign observers of British relations (for France and Germany: Terjanian; Köhnke; Lichtblau; for England and Scotland: Pocock; Hont; from a comparative perspective: Oz-Salzberger). Two good examples are the French Baron de Montesquieu and the London-based Dutch physician Bernard de Mandeville, both of whom readily appropriated the idea.

In its specifically British use, the term *doux commerce* expressed the conviction that the activities of buying, selling, bargaining and contracting caused individuals to engage with each other, even and especially in the presence of divergences of interest. Since mutual trust, respect, self-control and, of course, the renunciation of violence are elementary prerequisites of trade, it could be expected that an expansion of such relationships would put an end to arbitrary power relations. The generalisation of *commerce* would interest individuals in each other and cause them to treat each other with consideration and empathy. As a result, society as a whole would benefit. This view was brought to a wider audience when Joseph Addison, co-editor of the magazine *The Spectator* (1711-12, 1714), published a series of articles linking the argument of the beneficial effect of the market with an older discourse on *politeness* and *civility* conducted by aristocrats and wealthy citizens (cf. Knight 1993).

Journalistic support, however, does not explain the lasting acceptance of the figure of thought that remained dominant in England and – after the accession of Scotland in 1707 – the United Kingdom of Great Britain throughout the 18th century and, at most, faded slightly with the publication of Adam Smith's *Wealth of Nations* (1776), the 'Bible' of future economists. As Hirschman shows, as a description of the function and condition of civil society the ideal only went out of fashion around 1800 at the earliest. Only then did decidedly market-critical positions become more pronounced and a few decades later *doux commerce* at best enjoyed the attention of those who – like Herbert Spencer, one of the founding fathers of British sociology – specialised in researching exchange processes in social life (cf. Gray 171). The general acceptance of this market discourse in 18th-century Britain is all the more remarkable in view of the fact that foreign observers (with the exception of Montesquieu) mostly took a more critical attitude, and that the idea did not meet with the same broad approval as in the United Kingdom. While Georg Wilhelm Friedrich Hegel remained sceptical from the outset, Karl Marx ridiculed the whole idea of *doux commerce* (cf. Hirschman, *The Passions* 62; Rosanvallon 64).

For historians, as well as social scientists and scholars of cultural studies, Albert O. Hirschman's works on *commerce* and *doux commerce* are extraordinarily stimulating. This is because the author brought to life the common word used by contemporaries to describe the early modern market economy, *commerce*. Early modern economics in Britain cannot be sufficiently understood with contemporary, socio-scientifically constructed terms like "market" and "economy", which we use today and which are also in the title of this anthology. Although "market" was known as a noun and verb since the Middle Ages, it was used very unspecifically, and use of the term "economy" was still extremely rare. When Sir James Steuart published his pioneering work *Principles of Political Economy* (1767), he first had to laboriously remove the word from the context of the Greek word *oikos* (household), which was detrimental to the market success of his work. Seen in this light, Hirschman cut a path into the jungle of early modern economic history.

On the other hand, Hirschman's explanation for the ups and downs of *doux commerce* is too simple because, as can often be observed with economists, he drew conclusions from the theory of contemporary economists as evidence for what happened in practice. In this specific case, it amounts to saying that he attributed the turn away from *doux commerce* to the breakthrough of the Industrial Revolution and the triumph of capitalism. From a historical point of view, this is not convincing. The English economy had been a market economy long before 1800 and in this capacity had also developed capitalist elements. Tellingly, the time when the Enlightenment thinkers first put the idea of *doux commerce* down on paper was the period after the Glorious Revolution of 1688/89, when a genuinely capitalist institution like the Bank of England (1694) was founded and the financial markets of the City of London transformed the pound sterling into the capital that gave capitalism its name. Hirschman also relies on an outdated state of research with regard to the Industrial Revolution. In the 1970s, when he wrote *The Passions and the Interests*, economic historians did indeed still date the breakthrough to the 1780s. According to the current state of research, this can only be said for the period after about 1830; only then was commercial mass production, which had previously been decentralised and mostly rural (so-called proto-industry) production, moved to centralised factories on a large scale (cf., for example, King and Timmins). Thus, there is an unexplained chronological gap of around half a century in Hirschman's explanation, which must be bridged by other arguments.

This article attempts to bring the rise and fall of *doux commerce* into line with chronology. To this end it considers not only the history of markets and the market economy in Britain, but also the change of power relations in the social, political and media context in which they were embedded. In accordance with the focus of this volume, this article is limited to the British case. Following Albert O. Hirschman, this discussion aims to capture the complexity of civil society as a market society and thus raise the level of debate. In the context of this volume, this means at least alluding to the bridge to the "real fictions" of contemporary imagined economies.

THE RISE OF *COMMERCE* AND *DOUX COMMERCE*: BRITISH PECULIARITIES[1]

Early Start and Slow Pace of the Market Economy

Market relations, and by that I mean the exchange of goods and services for money, are probably as old as humanity. The prerequisite for their generalisation, however, is an institutional framework. In the case of England this framework was set up in 1066 when William the Conqueror defeated King Harold II at the Battle of Hastings. William liquidated almost the whole of the Anglo-Saxon nobility and declared himself lord

---

1 The explanations in the following chapter are based on the results of the research in Eisenberg, *The Rise of Market Society in England, 1066-1800*, unless otherwise stated. Therefore, I refrain from providing any further references.

of the territory which thereby became a unified state. The state was conducted on the basis of Common Law, a part continuation of Anglo-Saxon law. It was organised centrally, as far as that was possible with medieval means. The upshot was an economically and legally integrated territory with next to no internal customs control worth mentioning. Free persons, with the help of royal justice, were able to bring cases against fraudsters and bankrupt persons, lazy debtors and defaulting contractors. From 1362 at the latest they could even do so in the vernacular, because that was when English became the official language of administration. As currency the pound sterling was used as a continuation of Anglo-Saxon conventions. The old penny coins of the Anglo-Saxons were gradually replaced by new ones made of sterling silver.

In the early modern period, market relations continued to intensify. Agricultural labour markets became widespread after the plague wave of the 15th century, because the landlords were forced by the high demand for labour to relax feudal dependencies and accept freedom of movement. With the decline of the guilds in the 16th and 17th centuries free labour markets formed in many trades; sometimes even rudimentary trade unions sprang up to compensate for the structural disadvantages suffered by suppliers of labour. At about the same time, long-distance trade was intensified, equipping the consumer goods markets, which then assumed mass character in the 18th century, with the expansion of the proto-industrial mode of production in the countryside. A certain degree of underdevelopment in the banking sector was compensated for in 1694 by the founding of the Bank of England, which at the same time issued banknotes covered by tax revenues thus establishing a modern money market. The now flourishing financial markets favoured the financing of corporations and other larger enterprises, including the state, and with the South Sea Bubble in 1719/20, a first speculative crisis on a pan-European scale developed. Even in the longer term, individuals and collective financiers made substantial investments in the expansion of long-distance and domestic trade and infrastructure; wholesale and retail trade flourished, as did the press, entertainment and other service industries, both in urban and rural areas. Around 1800 market relationships in

England were so common that only minors and the inhabitants of poor-houses and other institutions were able to avoid the concomitant opportunities and demands. Every household made up at least one consumption unit (and quite often one production unit). In order to survive they were forced to deal with money. The simple exchange of natural goods and bartering was, if at all, widespread only among the inhabitants of far-flung villages.

Seen from such a long-term historical perspective, marketisation in England was characterised by several specific features. Firstly, the process began at an extraordinarily early date, at the end of the Middle Ages, and thence proceeded steadily without setbacks. If the individual stages of development created new social problems, they were rectified over time. Similarly, there was no accumulation of problems as a result of overlapping by other stages of modernisation. The nation state was in place before the domestic market took shape. The Industrial Revolution only began 750 years afterwards, when the market economy had already penetrated the entire British Isles. The fact that a brake was put on the dynamics of the English market society as a result of its early start and the gradual networking of business and society might be regarded as a problematic side-effect of the process. However, contemporaries did not regard this as a problem. As pioneers in the area they knew no other standards than their own. Thus the slow pace of development supported the perception of *commerce* as *doux commerce*.

Power Relations and Exchange Relations

In the process outlined, the Crown played a dual role. It guaranteed the framework conditions for free exchange, in which it was itself involved as an actor, and in the functioning of which it had a high degree of self-interest as it financed itself through tax revenues dependent on a flourishing community. To the extent that this dual role entailed contradictory requirements the Crown usually subordinated the ostentatious demonstration of its instruments of power to economic interests. Ever since the Magna Carta this priority has been evident in the recurrent negotiations between monarchs and parliament, which have always been occupied with the modalities of day-to-day market dealings. The extent of the willingness to renounce direct rule was evident not least in the military sphere. As early as the 12th century, the kings began to do without the active military service of the barons and instead imposed on them the costs of a mercenary army – a measure which in the long term meant that the English nobility no longer carried weapons but instead developed into a purely civilian landowning class. Especially in this measure medievalists recognise the basis of a specifically English "Bastard Feudalism" (McFarlane). A decisive mechanism for the early dissolution of personal dependencies was the fact that, unlike on the European continent, military service and other feudal services could, in principle, be performed in monetary form.

Another specific feature of the English feudal system was the lack of a graded hierarchy between king and subjects. In the interests of *divide et impera*, since William the Conqueror, the Crown took care to distribute baronial property throughout the land to prevent dynasties and conspiracies from developing. In their role as subjects of the Crown, the barons were on a par with the commoners, and when the Crown had monopolies to grant – and these included not only special rights of long-distance trading companies, but also e.g. entrepreneurs who acquired the right to hold markets in specific places – it awarded the contract to those who paid the highest price. Because of their formal equality as subjects, the English population was largely spared the negative experience of their contemporaries in early modern Central Europe, namely that in certain situations they became the object of power games of selfish intermediate instances of the ruling system, which – like city councils and guilds – were endowed with the authority of princes and local authorities and were able to enforce their particular interests at the expense of third parties (cf. Ogilvie, "The State in Germany" and *Institutions and European Trade*). In particular, they were spared from arbitrarily fixed feudal levies, bans on luxury and other restrictions on their economic activities, from restrictions on their rights as residents and citizens, from trading bans on certain population groups (e.g. foreigners and Jews) and finally from restrictions on their consumer behaviour. What that meant in everyday life becomes clear when we consider that Central European conventions of this kind also included the obligation of husbands to supervise the business of their wives and of master craftsmen to discipline apprentices and journeymen (cf. Ogilvie, "Consumption"; Kocka 329-34).

Insofar as English market actors coordinated themselves with the help of group action, organisation and consolidation of their capital in order to create a special basis of power in their respective economic environment, this was done on a voluntary and reciprocal basis. In this context it is worth mentioning the professionalisation efforts of insurance experts and stockbrokers, which during the course of the 18th century led to the creation of Lloyds of London and the London Stock Exchange; the turnpike societies and the private development companies to boost construction activity in the cities; the strikes and organisational efforts of journeymen; and finally, the countless friendly societies for mutual assistance in the event of illness and other dangers in a market society, which existed in all classes and strata of society. These coordinated activities not only yielded individual benefits, but also a number of welfare effects for society as a whole. All these features seemed to confirm the notion of *doux commerce*. Last but not least, one should mention popular culture with its sports competitions, games, theatre performances and concerts. The latter were extraordinarily lively and creative not least because voluntary associations and commercial initiatives were largely unaffected by interventions from the authorities and were therefore able to work together without hindrance.

Empathy as a Market Strategy

So far this article has attributed the experience of *doux commerce* in medieval and early modern England – firstly – to the guarantee of institutional framework conditions by the state and – secondly – to the weakness of feudal power structures, which might have impaired free market exchange. A third observation, which I would now like to elaborate on, refers to the necessity for market players in Britain to pay a great deal of attention to each other. This peculiarity was not, say, due to the fact that they only traded on a face-to-face basis or only with acquaintances, because even in the early modern era market relations were generally mediated by long chains of dealings and were therefore faced with all kinds of uncertainties. The decisive factor was rather that most transactions were not paid in cash, but with bills of exchange and promissory notes, i.e. written and personally signed orders. This convention had social consequences: because the inevitability of credit on a "good name" led to the fact that everyone was simultaneously a debtor and creditor, this made it necessary to have a high measure of self-promotion and sensitive external perception. The exchange economy was a reaction to the fact that the general shortage of coins in Europe was particularly pronounced in England, because, in order to preserve their autonomy externally, the monarchs had foreign coins rigorously confiscated and converted into pounds sterling. When Englishmen traded with each other they not only needed a good reputation, but were inevitably interested in the specific situation of their counterparts, which had to be investigated. Anyone who failed to submit to this effort – for example by insensitive haggling – ran the risk of harming his own reputation and cast doubt on his own creditworthiness. (cf. Muldrew).

Strategic *doux commerce* of this kind was particularly noticeable in the everyday dealings of the so-called "commercial classes", that is to say of the people who were professionally involved in shaping and co-ordinating market relationships. Contemporary statisticians counted the following among these: merchants, traders, agents and other so-called middlemen, exchange and share dealers, moneylenders, bankers and stock exchange workers. Then there was the so-called itinerant class by which I mean the armies of hauliers, mobile traders and representatives. And finally, there were also the hundreds of thousands of shopkeepers, whose influence on market activities reached a peak in the 17th and 18th centuries. We can include government civil servants involved in collecting taxes, members of professions like lawyers and notaries, publishers, journalists and those involved in the arts and entertainment. Many of these service people lived in growing towns which, in turn, created an additional need for coordination because of their complex social relationships. But one of the main features of English market society was that the thoroughly commercialised and regionally specialised agricultural business, which sold its produce at home and abroad, also relied heavily on go-between services.

Starting at the end of the 17th century, the number of connecting people of this kind grew rapidly and exchange relationships intensified. This was a further feature that motivated individuals to take an interest in each other; it also promoted the impression that commerce was a civilizing force. The growth had increased since the Middle Ages but received an above-average boost towards the start of the 18th century. Whereas between 1688 and 1750 the population grew by around 10%, the increase in the number of the above-mentioned professions – i.e. long before the start of industrialisation – was between 32 and 63% (de Vries and van der Woude 528-29).

Another measure of the outstanding importance of empathy as a market strategy of the "commercial classes" in early-modern England was the proportion of the service sector to the labour force. According to the 1801 census this comprised 34% of the economically active population, more than twice the figure in other countries in Western and Central Europe. Contemporaries regarded this as a problem of surplus supply, and their perception was clearly correct. For the order of magnitude of 34% was equivalent to the service sector of the USA around 1900 (32%), of the German Reich in 1936 (36%) and of France in 1937 (37%) (Buchheim 33). Anyone who offered services had to make an effort to ensnare his customers and clients, accommodate their interests and anticipate their expectations – features which were particularly relevant for personal services which comprised by far the largest sub-category.

Regarded in these terms, "doux commerce" in early-modern England was an expression and an effect of the existential competitive experiences of a surplus population which had been relieved of feudal duties and released into the duties and necessities of surviving in a market

society. Anyone arriving from the countryside in search of a job naturally tended to head in the direction of trading, transport and other activities in the service sector. And anyone either devoid of a viable business
idea or sufficient financial or social capital tried to get him- or herself a
paid job in one of these branches. Seen in this light, market actors in
early-modern England felt compelled to conduct their activities in the
sense of *doux commerce* particularly because their conditions of market
activities were anything but *doux*.

THE DECLINE OF *DOUX COMMERCE*

That concludes my argument that the idea of *doux commerce* had a real
basis in experience in early-modern England from which it drew its plau-
sibility. How do we now explain the fact that it waned in the 19th century? I ask this question because there was, as mentioned previously, not
only no change in direction or qualitative renewal of the process of marketisation in the decisive years around 1800, but also because one can
observe a large number of negative concomitants of the market society
before 1800 without, however, these facts taking centre-stage in the discourse. These include: speculation crises and irrational mass behaviour;
alienation; the accumulation of capital resources with its concomitant
accumulation of social power; and an increase in social inequality. I
would therefore like to propose explanations for the change in market
discourse that refer less to the economy itself than to the political and
social context it helped to shape.

One development which might contribute to explaining the decline
in the persuasive power of *doux commerce* is the structural change to
British public life between 1800 and 1830. The advance of a consumer
society in the 18th century had created new fashions at an ever increasing
rate, in clothing, household goods and other everyday objects; the act of
purchasing had been culturally inflated by the functional architecture of
businesses and commercial buildings and the attentive behaviour of
salespersons; and a commercial entertainment culture had reinvented

and perfected playful forms of expressions of market exchange in sport, theatre, music and other social activities. Fashion-makers, the advertising business and the enlightened press who mediated these attractions to an interested audience had first addressed the upper and middle classes, but the market principle extended beyond social boundaries. As far as consumption was concerned the lower strata of society and their interests were involved following the entanglement of luxury and second-hand markets as early as the 18th century (cf. Lemire), but these classes were scarcely taken into consideration in any debates on consumption.

As paying customers the lower classes were not regarded by journalists and public-relations experts as being sufficiently attractive to be a target group, because for many years they did not belong to the groups of buyers of newspapers, whose prices had been artificially increased by stamp duties, duties on paper and other taxes. These duties were, however, removed in the early 1830s and the first to profit were Chartist papers and the popular Penny Press. When wages began to increase as a result of the mid-Victorian boom, new types of newspapers aimed at a mass audience were launched onto the market. These competed for new classes of readers and therefore cooperated closely with other branches of the advertising industry (cf. Wiener). In this new competitive struggle journalists were unable to survive with *doux commerce* rhetoric. Much higher sales could be achieved by sensational stories about exploitation, blatant fraud and the negative effects of market failure (cf. Johnson; Taylor). A certain exception from the rule was the genre of "business journalism", represented for example by the *Economist;* as this was developed under the premise that it would be better to withhold certain details and practices of market exchange from public attention. This too was a contemporary adaptation of *doux commerce* to changed circumstances (cf. Poovey).

A second change in 19th century Britain, which I should like to put forward as an explanation for the waning of this idea, was the successful process of democratisation in Great Britain. In order to make this connection understandable it is helpful to recall a general difficulty when observing market exchange: the fact that the actors mostly administer their exit option tacitly. On the one hand, this can be explained by the fact that failed actors who leave the market do so tacitly. On the other hand, an alternative way of reacting, which might be described by Albert O. Hirschman as "voice", i.e. as "the act of complaining or organising oneself ... with the intention of achieving a direct improvement of quality," presupposes a concrete addressee, and such a person or group of persons cannot be identified in markets – in contrast to organisations or other hierarchical settings (Hirschman, "Abwanderung" 332-33, trans. by Eisenberg; cf. Hirschman, *Exit, Voice, and Loyalty* 22-25). In the 17th and 18th centuries, this frustration often led to collective protests, say, against a rise in prices often being aimed at the nearest addressees, which at the time were mostly local political authorities. Edward P. Thompson has described this vividly in his work on the "moral economy" of the crowd. When, in the wake of the French Revolution, radical politics discovered Parliament as the place to address demands and protests, this created a new sounding board for "voice": one whose comprehensive scope corresponded to the nationwide dimension of commercial society. The political movements in the 19th century, from the London Corresponding Society via Chartism, the trade union and cooperative movements all the way to the Reform Movement, then took the next step by feeding concepts like 'exploitation', 'inequality' and 'class' into market discourse. It is irrelevant whether these concepts alone were new or described the situation at hand correctly. It is much more important to realise that these new public emphases were highly appropriate to express doubts about the integrating capacity of markets in civil society (cf. Noel Thompson; Hobsbawm; Stedman Jones).

This effect was bolstered by concrete experiences which also extended beyond local levels. With the help of strikes and the collective use of economies of scale, trade unions and consumer cooperatives, which operated at national levels from the 1860s onward, succeeded in intervening in the power relationships of labour and consumer markets. This changed public perceptions to such an extent that they were now seen as representatives of the interests of market victims. The foundation of the Labour Party at the turn of the 20th century finally brought the social question onto the main political stage. As a result, the negotiation of explicit rules of interaction between market actors was subjected more than ever to the imperatives of political elections and political parties, which sought to create a mass appendage under the impression of the ever-expanding right to vote. However, the pioneer of this type of mass party, which included this in their calculations, was the Chartist Movement of the 1830s, which was the first to make free and universal (male) suffrage its banner and thus set the standards for others to come. Although the Chartists failed, they greatly accelerated the transformation of the old Whig Party into the Liberal Party and the Tories into the Conservative Party, as well as the demand for participation in the general press. The rules and expectations of conduct that specific social groups wanted to generalise were now the subject of controversial discussion and made the potential for social conflict more apparent than before (cf. Searle; Johnson).

The more these processes of democratisation progressed, the paler the idea of *doux commerce* became and soon it disappeared completely from public discourse. On the one hand, it was hardly possible to convey to the general public that the market that gave rise to such disputes could prompt members of civil society to conduct themselves with self-control, respect and mutual trust. Towards the end of the 19th century, the central question of market discourse to the British public was therefore no longer "How can markets, how can commerce contribute to fending off arbitrary claims to power brought to society from outside", but "Why do markets threaten civil society from within?" (Keane 30). On the other hand, the market became the subject of an expert discourse. Parliamentary and journalistic debates on stock speculation, liability obligations of partnerships, employee profit-sharing and the right of coalition led to a number of new laws, and some industrialists adopted high-profile initiatives on company social policy. This development profiled the opportunities of corporate market actors and took the experience-based perspectives of individuals off the agenda. This was not least at the expense of consumers, who had always experienced *doux commerce* to a special degree and were now moved to the margins of public discourse (this is the argument of Parry 164-86, especially 185; see also Searle 264-68; and Johnson).

COMMERCE AND DOUX COMMERCE
IN THE LONG-TERM PERSPECTIVE

The market was traditionally seen as a place where real people met to exchange and do business – a place for *commerce* and *doux commerce* alike. This interactive, sociable dimension of the market had been particularly pronounced in Britain since the Middle Ages, probably stronger than in continental European countries that I have not examined further in this paper. But in Britain, too, it increasingly faded into the background over the course of the 19th century, with the result that *doux commerce* as a figure of thought became obsolete. At least when Hirschman reintroduced it into economic discourse in the 1970s and 1980s, it had been widely forgotten, and it has remained so. Even the collapse of Soviet-style socialism, which gave the market economy an unexpected boost and legitimacy, did not change this state of affairs. When the political scientist and philosopher John Keane, a proven leftist, introduced the first issue of the *Journal of Civil Society* at the beginning of the 21st century with an homage to this old idea, he did so as a deliberate provocation to ignite a controversy. But some of the contributors from other European countries reacted so sharply that the debate was nipped in the bud.

The historical processes underlying this development are obvious: when it is not a question of selling a highly specialised workforce or buying houses or used cars, today's market players are confronted with fixed prices that make bargaining superfluous. The legislator has standardised contracting, and the interactions required for transactions are increasingly carried out through computers and other vending machines. This has further weakened the imagination of the commercial society and the possibilities for shaping it. *Commerce* has definitely disappeared from the scientific as well as the general political discourse. The substitute term "market", on the other hand, is in its typical uses an empty abstraction, even a phantom, which can be imagined at will.

Accordingly, current research in this field is largely limited to technical questions like examining the market pricing mechanism or individual responses to the challenge of uncertainty. It is mostly about the efficiency of either "the economy" or "capitalism". The cultural-studies correlate of this type of 'market research' are analyses of "fictions" and "real fictions" of the market, as collected in this volume. This opens up a new, original field of experimentation for critical researchers. However, in most research of this kind the term "market" typically refers to an abstraction, indeed a phantom, whose quality and scope are time-spanning. What is missing is a historicisation of the modes of linking "reality" and "fiction" of the market. It is difficult to imagine how the gap between economics and economic life could be overcome without such an analysis.

REFERENCES

Buchheim, Christoph. *Industrielle Revolution. Langfristige Wirtschafts-entwicklung in Großbritannien, Europa und Übersee.* Deutscher Taschenbuch Verlag, 1994.

Eisenberg, Christiane. *The Rise of Market Society in England, 1066-1800.* Translated by Deborah Cohen, Berghahn Publishers, 2013.

Gray, Tim. *The Political Philosophy of Herbert Spencer.* Avebury, 1996.

Hirschman, Albert O. *The Passions and the Interests. Political Arguments for Capitalism before its Triumph.* Princeton University Press, 1977.

—. *Exit, Voice, and Loyalty. Responses to Decline in Firms, Organizations and States.* Harvard University Press, 1970.

—. "Abwanderung, Widerspruch und das Schicksal der Deutschen Demokratischen Republik: Ein Essay zur konzeptuellen Geschichte." *Leviathan*, vol. 20, no. 3, 1992, pp. 330-58.

—. "Rival Interpretations of Market Society: Civilizing, Destructive, or Feeble?" *Journal of Economic Literature*, vol. 20, 1982, pp. 1463-84.

Hirschman, Daniel Abramson. *Inventing the Economy. Or: How We Learned to Stop Worrying and Love the GDP*. PhD Thesis University of Michigan, 2016.

Hobsbawm, Eric. "Soziale Ungleichheiten und Klassenstrukturen in England: Die Arbeiterklasse." *Klassen in der europäischen Sozialgeschichte*, edited by Hans-Ulrich Wehler, Vandenhoeck & Ruprecht, 1979, pp. 53-65.

Hont, Istvan. "The Language of Sociability and Commerce: Samuel Pufendorf and the Theoretical Foundations of the 'Four States Theory'." *The Languages of Political Theory in Early-Modern Europe*, edited by Anthony Pagden, Cambridge University Press, 1987, pp. 253-76.

Johnson, Paul. *Making the Market. Victorian Origins of Corporate Capitalism*. Cambridge University Press, 2010.

Keane, John. "Eleven Theses on Markets and Civil Society." *Journal of Civil Society*, vol. 1, 2005, pp. 25-34.

King, Steven, and Geoffrey Timmins. *Making Sense of the British Industrial Revolution. English Economy and Society*. Manchester University Press, 2001.

Knight, Charles A. "The Spectator's Moral Economy." *Modern Philology*, vol. 91, no. 2, 1993, pp. 161-79.

Kocka, Jürgen. *Arbeitsverhältnisse und Arbeiterexistenzen. Grundlagen der Klassenbildung im 19. Jahrhundert*. Dietz, 1990.

Köhnke, Karl Christian. "Art. 'Verkehr'." *Historisches Wörterbuch der Philosophie*, edited by V. Joachim Ritter, vol. 11, Wissenschaftliche Buchgesellschaft, 2001, pp. 704-05.

Lemire, Beverly. *The Business of Everyday Life. Gender, Practice and Social Politics in England, c. 1600-1900*. Manchester University Press, 2005.

Lichtblau, Klaus. "Art. 'Vergesellschaftung'." *Historisches Wörterbuch der Philosophie*, edited by V. Joachim Ritter, vol. 11, Wissenschaftliche Buchgesellschaft, 2001, pp. 666-71.

McFarlane, Kenneth Bruce. "Parliament and Bastard Feudalism." *Transactions of the Royal Historical Society*, 4th series, vol. 26, 1944, pp. 53-79.

Mitchell, Timothy. *Rule of Experts. Egypt, Techno-Politics, Modernity.* University of California Press, 2002.

Muldrew, Craig. *The Economy of Obligation: The Culture of Credit and Social Relations Early Modern England.* Palgrave Macmillan, 1998.

Ogilvie, Sheilagh. *Institutions and European Trade. Merchant Guilds, 1000-1800.* Cambridge University Press, 2011.

—. "Consumption, Social Capital, and the 'Industrious Revolution' in Early Modern Germany." *The Journal of Economic History*, vol. 70, no. 2, 2010, pp. 287-325.

—. "The State in Germany. A Non-Prussian View." *Rethinking Leviathan. The Eighteenth-Century State in Britain and Germany*, edited by John Brewer and Eckhart Hellmuth, Oxford University Press for the German Historical Institute, 1999, pp. 167-201.

Oz-Salzberger, Fania. "Scots, Germans, Republic and Commerce." *Republicanism. A Shared European Heritage*, edited by Martin van Gelderen and Quentin Skinner, vol. 2, Cambridge University Press, 2002, pp. 197-226.

Parry, Jonathan. "The Decline of Institutional Reform in Nineteenth-Century Britain." *Structures and Transformations in Modern British History*, edited by David Feldman and Jon Lawrence, Cambridge University Press, 2011, pp. 164-86.

Pocock, John G. A. *Virtue, Commerce, and History: Essays on Political Theory, Chiefly in the Eighteenth Century.* Cambridge University Press, 1985.

Poovey, Mary. "Writing about Finance in Victorian England: Disclosure and Secrecy in the Culture of Investment." *Victorian Investments: New Perspectives on Finance and Culture*, edited by Nancy Henry and Cannon Schmitt, Indiana University Press, 2009, pp. 39-57.

Porter, Roy. "The New Eighteenth-Century Social History." *Culture and Society in Britain 1660-1800*, edited by Jeremy Black, Manchester University Press, 1997, pp. 29-50.

Rosanvallon, Pierre. *Le Capitalisme utopique. Histoire de l'idée de marché*. Éditions du Seuil, 1979.

Searle, Geoffrey. *Morality and the Market in Victorian Britain*. Clarendon Press, 1998.

Stedman Jones, Gareth. "The Language of Chartism." *The Chartist Experience: Studies in Working-Class Radicalism and Culture, 1830-60*, edited by James Epstein and Dorothy Thompson, Macmillan, 1982, pp. 3-58.

Steuart, James. *An Inquiry into the Principles of Political Oeconomy being an Essay on the Science of Domestic Policy in Free Nations, in which are Particularly Considered Population, Agriculture, Trade, Industry, Money, Coin, Interest, Circulation, Banks, Exchange, Public Credit, and Taxes*. Printed for A. Millar and T. Cadell, in the Strand, 1767.

Taylor, James. *Creating Capitalism. Joint-Stock Enterprise in British Politics and Culture, 1800-1870*. Royal Historical Society in association with the Boydell Press, 2006.

Terjanian, Anoush Fraser. *'Doux Commerce' and its Discontents: Slavery, Piracy and Monopoly in Eighteenth-Century France*. Ph.D. Thesis University of Baltimore, 2005.

Thompson, Edward P. *Customs in Common. Studies in Traditional Popular Culture*. The New Press, 1991.

Thompson, Noel. *The Market and its Critic Socialist Political Economy in Nineteenth-Century Britain*. Routledge, 1988.

Vries, Jan de, and Ad van der Woude. *The First Modern Economy. Success, Failure and Perseverance of the Dutch Economy, 1500-1815*. Cambridge University Press, 1997.

Wiener, Joel H. "How New was the New Journalism?" *Papers for the Millions: The New Journalism in Britain, 1850 to 1914*, edited by Joel H. Wiener, Greenwood Press, 1988, pp. 47-71.

The Emotional Economies of Colonial Capitalism and Its Legacies

Jana Gohrisch

INTRODUCTION

In his essay "Imagined, Real and Moral Economies" published in 2014, John Clarke defines 'imagined' as "the discursive or ideological representation of what an economy is" (97). In his contribution to this volume "Why *Imagined* Economies?" he uses the term interchangeably with 'imaginary' as a device to escape the dominant neoliberal narrative of 'the Economy' and to open up intellectual space "for imagining other economies, or even for imagining economies otherwise" (see chapter Clarke in this volume). However, neither text employs the categories race and ethnicity, which are as central as class (and gender) to understand how, since the onset of large-scale colonisation, capitalist agricultural and industrial enterprises owned mainly by whites have managed to enlist the state and public funding to secure cheap black and brown labour to make private profit. An equally unacknowledged white perspective predominates in Ute Frevert's introduction and survey essay in her edited collection *Moral Economies*. Despite the focus on the – slave-trading – 18th century that comes with her topic, she mentions colonialism and enslavement as means of accumulating capital only in passing

(Frevert, "Moral Economies" 20, 37, 39). Both Frevert and Clarke, however, borrow E. P. Thompson's term 'moral economy' to understand past and present economic thought. While Frevert refutes Thompson's politics and eventually uses the term very generally to specify the "conflicting views on economic activities" (Frevert, "Introduction" 11), Clarke treats "'moral economies' as another form of imagined economy" ("Imagined, Real" 95). He employs Thompson's ideas as a springboard to reflect convincingly on "whether the moral, political and economic can – and should – be related" today (107).[1]

Taking literally the second half of this volume's title, real fictions, I will read the colonial novel *Lutchmee and Dilloo. A Study of West Indian Life* (1877) by Edward Jenkins, a British writer and political reformer, to highlight the connections between race, class and the economy from the perspective of literary studies. With this, I wish to extend the interdisciplinary discussion of imagined economies into the past, thus complementing Melissa Kennedy's literary studies contribution to this volume. She investigates the potential of the arts and humanities "to intervene in education, public discourse, and economic decision-making" (see chapter Kennedy in this volume) for which she conjures up a contemporary 'we' to imagine a collective subject in opposition to neoliberal capitalism. In my chapter, however, I propose to acknowledge the conflicting interests of the distinctly racialised agents in capitalist economy and, from there, to understand the cognitive and emotional effects

---

1   Clarke writes: "Thompson's use of the idea [of a moral economy] was located in a specific social formation and its disruption, producing a moment in which food rioters in 18th century England laid claim to collective understandings of how economic relations were structured by moral obligations. Rioters – and those who judged them – understood this field of moral ties as legitimation for public anger and action. The current instabilities of the dominantly imagined economy have made it more possible to pose questions about questions of whether the moral, political and economic can – and should – be related." (107)

of these unresolved conflicts in both quotidian and academic discourses today.

Lutchmee and Dilloo. A Study of West Indian Life is set in British Guyana's sugar plantation economy of the 1870s and is, despite the investigative connotations of 'study', marked out as 'real fiction' by its generically mixed aesthetics. It is a work of artistic imagination self-confidently embedded in British economic imperialism and its concomitant racist colonial ideology. I argue that the novel establishes a racialised emotional economy to normalise the extensive exploitation of underpaid brown and black migrant labour for its implied white middle-class and metropolitan readership. To take the argument further, this normalising discourse has had both epistemological and emotional repercussions in Britain, which continues to shape the debate about economy and race to this very day. The most conspicuous legacies of the emotional economies of colonial capitalism are a select epistemological silence and an equally select emotional eloquence. Together, they serve to disconnect what is causally connected: capitalist economy and racist discrimination.

LEGACIES IN 21ST-CENTURY NON-FICTION: EITHER ECONOMY OR RACE

Neither the British sociologist (John Clarke), the German historian (Ute Frevert) nor the literary studies scholar based in Austria (Melissa Kennedy) quoted above mentions race (although the latter has published widely on colonial capitalism). Neither do the two US-American representatives of economic criticism, a relatively new approach in literary criticism, as they dismiss the category to a footnote (Woodmansee and

Osteen 43). Conversely, if one takes a look at the long history of American Critical Race Theory[2], race is central, but one finds little to no fundamental censure of capitalist economy when practised by whites. To this field Nancy Leong has recently added a substantial essay on "Racial Capitalism" published in the specialist *Harvard Law Review*. Similar to Eva Illouz's critique of the commodification of emotions and their transformation into "emodities" (Illouz 1ff.), Leong analyses the commercialisation of non-white racial identities. She then suggests legal measures to ameliorate the detrimental effects of this process on African and white Americans alike.

Targeting a much larger audience in Britain, award-winning journalist Reni Eddo-Lodge and former barrister-turned-journalist Afua Hirsch, popular historian David Olusoga, and rapper Akala (to name but a few) write about race in late-capitalist Britain. They keep a high profile on the internet with blogs, videos and websites as well as in other media, especially documentary and educational film. Eddo-Lodge has won several awards; Hirsch was one of the judges for the 2019 Booker Prize; and Olusoga is a much sought-after writer, broadcaster, TV presenter and filmmaker who, through his work, has continuously drawn attention to the importance of race in Britain. While the tone of the academics mentioned above is emotionally detached, with some irony added in Clarke, the journalists opt for emotional display to make themselves heard and, ironically, seen.

More than 30 years ago, Paul Gilroy published his antiracist polemic *There Ain't No Black in the Union Jack. The Cultural Politics of Race*

---

2   The overwhelmingly rich African American discussion of race is not part of my discussion but there is plenty of material dissecting the intricate connections between race and the economy which, to name just one seminal text, Angela Davis's Women, Race and Class (1981) shows. For an antiracist critique of Gender Studies see Sabine Broeck's Gender and the Abjection of Blackness (2018). See also her co-edited collection (with Jason R. Ambroise) Black Knowledges/Black Struggles: Essays in Critical Epistemology (2015).

and Nation (1987). It is one of the most outstanding in a long line of similar texts that have come out since the end of the 20ᵗʰ century and the millennium, when New Labour's policy of multiculturalism encouraged fictional and non-fictional writing by black and Asian British writers. Why should two young black British professional women (Eddo-Lodge, Hirsch) see the need to cover the same ground again and to such public acclaim? Fred D'Aguiar, Guyana-born writer and critic of the Gilroy-generation, explains the reason in a fictive letter to Beryl Gilroy, the Guyanese-British author of the autobiographical *Black Teacher* (1994) and mother of Paul Gilroy. 15 years after her death, D'Aguiar honours her brave struggle against frequent occurrences of institutional and everyday racism. Employing an economic metaphor, he deplores with some bitterness that Beryl Gilroy had fought "without an insurance policy against their reoccurrence" ("Letter to Beryl Gilroy" 759). He continues: "It is this sad and dismaying reality which informs racism in Britain, that it is ever lasting, that the vigilance against it must be a perpetual stance, never to be relaxed and certainly never retired from use." (759) Subsequently, D'Aguiar retraces his bold statement made 30 years earlier when he provocatively opened an essay with the claim: "There is no Black British literature, there is only literature with its usual variants of class, sex, race, time and place." ("Against Black British" 106) Despite the fact that the "bigger white-owned presses have cashed in on the demand for black creativity" (111), he states in his letter to Beryl Gilroy that black British writers "feel that Britishness obliterates difference rather than seeing difference in others as an enrichment of it" ("Letter to Beryl Gilroy" 761). He mentions public administration, police and prisons explicitly as places of racism (759) but not the economy.

Afua Hirsch and Reni Eddo-Lodge differ in their registers from both the earlier writers and from each other. Hirsch's *Brit(ish): On Race, Identity and Belonging* is a generic mixture of memoir, reportage and political analysis, which comes across as personally concerned but calm and reflective. Situated at the other end of the emotional spectrum, Eddo-Lodge adopts a belligerent stance occasionally resorting to anger and rage as evident in the book's sarcastic title *Why I'm No Longer Talking to White People about Race* taken from a blog posted in 2014. Although the two writers are explicit on the imperial origins and economic implications of British racism and refer to the large-scale economically motivated immigration after the war, they do not discuss the causal and structural links between the neoliberal economy and racial discrimination. Both, however, comment on social class. Afua Hirsch is very much aware of her middle-class status and privilege, especially in contrast to black working-class people, which allow her to explore her identity as a mixed-race professional woman. Despite this economic belonging, she feels emotionally excluded from British society. Based on statistics and census data, Reni Eddo-Lodge exposes the phrase 'white working class' as a construct in the tradition of 'divide and rule' (Eddo-Lodge 95-96, 202, 206) designed to remove from sight black and brown working-class people.

Both writers forcefully denounce that, "in Britain, we are taught not to see race" (Hirsch 10). Eddo-Lodge spells out the consequences: "Colour-blindness does not accept the legitimacy of structural racism or a history of white racial dominance. [...] In order to dismantle unjust, racist structures, we must see race" (Eddo-Lodge 83-84). Hirsch ends her book with the following caveat: "Colour [...] blindness [...] is not a good strategy for seeing what is there. Race is there, as lived experience, as the basis for the most dramatic economic and human shifts in history" (318). While Hirsch uses the adjective 'economic', Eddo-Lodge explains racism more generally as "the survival strategy of systemic power" (64). She convincingly contends that racism is not "about moral values" (64) but then does not spell out what 'systemic power' would comprise in her view. Similar to Hirsch's style, her diction shows a preference for passive constructions and abstract references to 'structure' and 'system'. Alluding to her (unwillingly taken) role as "the angry black woman" (186), she declares: "I have no desire to be equal. I want to deconstruct the structural power of a system that marked me out as different. [...] Equality is fine as a transitional demand but [...] it is the easy route" (184). Eddo-Lodge's argument leaves the reader to choose from two imagined camps: white, dominant and complacent or black, oppressed and angry. "[R]acism is a white problem. It reveals the anxieties, hypocrisies and double standards of whiteness. It is a problem in the psyche of whiteness that white people must take responsibility to solve" (219). Eddo-Lodge then warns of pointless "white guilt" and demands: "Instead, get angry. Anger is useful. Use it for good" (221). I shall now take up Eddo-Lodge's call indicating the agents and their conflicting interests in the economic processes that constitute the systemic power she condemns.

MID-19TH-CENTURY COLONIAL FICTION: ECONOMY, RACE, EMOTIONS

Someone who unashamedly 'sees' race, as well as the hierarchies of class and ethnicity, and openly presents them as pillars of 19th-century imperial economy is Edward Jenkins (1838-1910). The once well-known writer disappeared from view for most of the 20th century and was only rediscovered by postcolonial-studies scholars in the 21st century enquiring into the role of indenture in post-emancipation Caribbean economies.

After the abolition of slavery in the British Empire in 1833, the former slave-owners, especially in the newer colonies of Trinidad and Guyana, imported migrant labourers mainly from India and China to replace the Africans who left the industrial plantation economy due to oppressive conditions and low wages. "Between 1838 and 1918, approximately 500,000 Indians and 200,000 Chinese were brought to work in the Caribbean [...]" (Klein 4). Describing the situation for Guyana, Brian Moore specifies the exact numbers and hints at the tax-based financial arrangements underpinning the process: "By 1900 a total of 270,448 immigrants, nearly three times the native [African-Guyanese] population of 1838, were brought into the colony at public expense: from Madeira 32,216 [...], from India 210,639, from Africa 14,060, and from China 13,533" (Moore 8). In order to escape their impoverished conditions in colonial India following massive displacements especially in the provinces of Bihar, Bengal and Madras (Klein 67), thousands of Indian peasants and small artisans agreed to contracts offering five years of badly but steadily paid plantation work in the Caribbean. In Guyana, "the planter-dominated colonial regime" spent "large sums of public money to import new immigrant labourers" (Moore 8) which "conflicted directly with the interests of the native Creoles" whose "wages fell" as "jobs became scarcer, taxation to support immigration rose" (Moore 11) and land became more difficult to acquire. The British state, that is the Colonial Office, administered the process through its representatives in London and the colonies such as Guyana. "The state was responsible for protecting the economic interests of the plantations, as well as the social and political interests of the white minority" (Moore 13). State-paid governors, administrators, magistrates and other staff made sure the local colonial economies ran smoothly. After the Second World War, the British state was once again responsible for the supply of cheap labour for British businesses as well as British public services, such as transport and the NHS, and achieved this by importing large contingents of workers from the Caribbean in the 1950s and 1960s, followed by South Asians in the 1960s and 1970s. These are similar processes based on the same racist principle: state-managed import of cheap black and brown labour to serve the needs of privately (but also welfare state-) owned white businesses.

In 1870 Jenkins, then a liberal MP and barrister, went to British Guyana on behalf of the London-based Aboriginal Protection and Anti-Slavery Society to report on the work of a royal commission investigating the conditions of indentured labourers on the sugar plantations. In 1871, he published the comprehensive study *The Coolie. His Rights and Wrongs* with which he calls for more state control over the plantation owners' abusive treatment of their workforce.[3] As the text had not stirred

---

3   The cover and title page of the 1871 American edition advertised the text as "By the Author of Ginx's Baby" instead of giving the author's name. Letizia Gramaglia used this edition for the re-publication of The Coolie. His Rights

the British public into the pity and compassion Jenkins wished it to feel for the Indian labourers' plight, he took to fiction to popularise the matter. By then, he was already famous for his satires *Ginx's Baby* and *Little Hodge*, two slim volumes, which today make for annoying reading compared to the great tradition of English satire. They are both condescending in tone and conservative in politics because they suggest that the working and the peasant classes are in need of help by the middle and upper classes. The latter, however, do nothing but meddle incompetently with the affairs of the poor instead of alleviating their sufferings.[4] Published after the two satires, *Lutchmee and Dilloo. A Study of West Indian Life* was widely reviewed in the British quality press. A search in the British Library Newspapers Database yields at least eleven longer reviews and many more short notices, which suggest that the novel was indeed read – even if not always favourably. A good summary of the general opinion appeared in the Cardiff-based *Western Mail*, whose reviewer juxtaposes *Lutchmee and Dilloo* with Jenkins's earlier writings to conclude:

> "Lutchmee and Dilloo" [...] is a dreadfully weary and ill-structured tale, and I should think would find no more favour with the public than his account of the results of the commission of inquiry in British Guiana on the same subject. Whatever little reputation Mr. Jenkins has derived from "Ginx's Baby"

---

and Wrongs in The Guyana Classics Library in 2010 to which she also contributed an introduction.

4   The following editions of Ginx's Baby sold well, not least because the cover carried one of the most famous photographs of the 1870s, which represents an enraged toddler. Charles Darwin himself had commissioned the picture from the controversial art photographer Oscar Gustav Rejlander for his study The Expression of the Emotions in Man and Animals (1872). Neither Darwin nor Rejlander ever disclosed that the latter had seriously modified the image to bring out better the anger and pain of the depicted infant. The photographer not only sold the picture to the popular press but also in its hundreds of thousands as carte(s)-de-visite (Smith 226).

will not long survive such pitiable literary efforts as "Lutchmee and Dilloo".
("London Correspondence")

On the other side of the evaluative spectrum resides *Lloyd's Weekly Newspaper* whose reviewer calls the novel an "admirable work" because it will stir the otherwise complacent readers of Mudie's Lending Library into some awareness of injustice ("Literature"). While this review offers Jenkins "hearty thanks" for having "striven valiantly on behalf of the coolies", *The Saturday Review*, reflecting the taste of well-educated readers, falls in with the verdict passed by the *Western Mail*. "Meanwhile no good will be done to the coolie by writing third-rate sensational novels about him" ("Lutchmee and Dilloo" 720). Other reviews repeatedly problematise Jenkins's purpose, such as the *London Society*, a magazine dedicated to "light and amusing literature for the hours of relaxation", which sharply quips: "Mr. Jenkins is a novelist who always writes with a purpose, and what he gains in purpose he frequently loses in the construction of the story" ("New Books" 565). Having pointed out twice the "exaggerated" tone of Jenkins's novels and of *Lutchmee and Dilloo* in particular (565), the reviewer in the end praises the "many scenes of pathos and eloquence" (565-66) which he obviously deems fit for his readers' "hours of relaxation". F. M. Owen, writing for *The Academy*, an intellectual weekly dedicated to raising the quality of fiction, has no desire to cover up the novel's failure, attributing this to "its subject, the wrongs of the Coolies in Demerara", which he thinks "is inartistic" (Owen 547). Like most of the other reviewers, he speculates about the readers' feeling sympathy for Dilloo but not "sufficient interest in the story as a story to pursue it, except from a high sense of philanthropic duty" (547). Unsurprisingly, *The Athenaeum* and *The Saturday Review*, the two leading review journals with famous writers as reviewers, offer the most scathing criticism of the novel's failed aesthetics: "the reader feels that there is something wrong somewhere" ("Literature: Novels of the Week" 491). *The Athenaeum* points to Jenkins's problematic use of sources mixing Mauritius with Guyana, which gives the novel an air of "unreality" ("Literature: Novels of the Week" 491), while *The Saturday*

Review, with ironic verve, draws attention to Jenkins's free copying from a variety of Blue Books, especially on Barbados ("Lutchmee and Dilloo" 719). Both reviewers systematically discuss the novel's shortcomings with regard to plot, character, description and dialogue, drawing attention to striking contradictions. Instead of the Uncle-Tom style indictment of the hardships of indenture, expected by the reviewers, the novel presents an improbably well-off major Indian character and individual white mismanagement as cause for some merely minor injustices ("Literature: Novels of the Week" 491). Moreover, the reviewers criticise the novel's unconvincing presentation of the Indian characters' feelings ("Lutchmee and Dilloo" 720). Taken together, the reviews document that the novel was widely read across the social spectrum and variously appreciated or rejected depending on the journals' inscribed readership. None of the reviewers, however, finds fault with imperial economics based on contract labour. Yet, it is this system that Jenkins deems useful for the exploited workers if only administered properly. Thus, he writes in the preface to his novel:

> I have long since expressed the opinion that a Coolie system, under proper supervision and restraint, could be made a system of incalculable benefit to the Asiatics. But the sole condition on which we can allow it to exist within our dominions is that our Government shall exercise over it […] most rigid control. (Jenkins 29)

Jenkins was "a staunch British imperialist" (Sutherland 330, Graves and Milne) but "no clichéd" one (Dabydeen 8). The few literary critics who read the novel today welcome it – despite its shortcomings and obvious racism – as the first literary representation of Indian indentured labourers (Dabydeen, Jackson, Klein, Poynting). Indo-Guyanese novelist and critic David Dabydeen has made possible the only two existing re-editions of *Lutchmee and Dilloo*: in 2003, in the Caribbean Classics series of Macmillan Education, introduced by himself, and in 2010, in The Guyana Classics Library, with him as general editor. In the preface to the series, financed by the Government of Guyana, Bharrat Jagdeo, then

President of Guyana, honours Jenkins's novel as the "only substantial fiction on Guiana [sic]" in the 19th century (Jagdeo v). The series' aim is that "all Guyanese can appreciate our monumental achievement in moving from Exploitation to Expression" (vi). How exactly would this work with Jenkins's novel, which expresses exploitation in a way that makes it inexpressible and thus acceptable, as I shall reveal shortly? The answer lies in the very mode of expression it selects, in its imagined emotional economy, which functions by derailing and re-directing anger and its concomitant cognitions[5] of discontent and resentment to render it harmless. It is here that the emotional economy of colonial capitalism differs from the 'moral economy' E. P. Thompson found operating in 18th-century England on its transition to capitalist market economy. Relying on a wealth of historical sources he studied how the lower classes successfully transformed their "fury for corn" (Thompson 135), especially in times of dearth, into meaningful action by threatening riots to force the prices for corn down. "This fury for corn is a curious culmination of the age of agricultural improvement. [...] The breakthrough of the new political economy of the free market was also the breakdown of the old moral economy of provision" (Thompson 135-36). In the following, I will look at the management of fury and anger in fiction, taking the concern with real history onto the level of representation and thus imagination.

---

5   The cognitive components of emotions refer to the perception of internal states and external stimuli, that is, they comprise the processes of evaluating, digesting, remembering and controlling emotions on the part of the individual (Ulich and Mayring 51).

MANAGING ANGER
IN THE IMAGINED PLANTATION ECONOMY
OF *LUTCHMEE AND DILLOO*

Whose anger does the novel select for representation? How does the text embed anger situationally? Which material and immaterial objects are evaluated by the emotion, that is, what is the aim of the anger? Which are its dominant cognitions and how does the text manage their display? How does the novel link anger to its imagined economy?

The novel's first five (of the 59) chapters are set in India. It begins with Lutchmee, the light-brown and beautiful female protagonist, who is sexually harassed by Hunoomaun, the dark-brown village watchman and long-standing opponent to Lutchmee's "manly" but "low-caste" husband Dilloo (Jenkins 34, 36). Lutchmee is saved first by Dilloo and then by the British deputy magistrate, whose wife she serves as a maid after Dilloo has left for Guyana. Not only does the novel imagine the white colonisers as protectors of the jealously warring natives but it also keeps quiet about the ravages of colonising rural India that cause emigration in the first place. Instead of hinting at the economic changes, which drive men like Dilloo away, the novel blames dark-skinned Hunoomaun, typified as "ugly" (36), "villainous" (36, 90) and, later, as "cowardly" (97-98), for destroying his opponent's crop and stealing his savings (37-38). The following chapter offers a way out by introducing an over-paid and manipulative recruiter whose promises lure Dilloo to Guyana, where the three Indians meet again as contract labourers on a sugar plantation.

What seems a mere exposition turns out to be a most effective narrative technique to derail anger, rage and wrath, the disruptive emotions the authorial narrator attributes to both white planters and brown labourers, on both sides of the economic divide in Guyana. This character-centred device serves to contain the economically caused social conflicts within an epically told tale of individual jealousy and revenge. The "revenge tragedy" (Poynting 218) culminates in a deadly fight between the two labourers, described in detail at the end of the novel, in which Dilloo kills his opponent. In accordance with the genre conventions (to which the villain also belongs) and with contemporary racist notions of the non-white other, the narrator stereotypically refers to Dilloo's "passionate nature" (Jenkins 252) and "resentful passion" (279). He then presents him as melodramatically promising his wife: "'I will live only to revenge myself on those who have done us wrong, on the cursed tyrants who here enslave and torment us; and [...] I, Dilloo, will give myself to work only for their destruction, worry, and death!'" (253). Jenkins's text immediately re-directs this anger by replacing its object, although it had shown at length that the anger was justified as Dilloo had to serve time in jail due to a corrupt interpreter and law court (173ff.). Instead of overpowering economic and legal "tyrants", Dilloo merely fights a single man of his own social, racial and ethnic group. Thus, the only destruction Dilloo brings about, apart from Hunoomaun's, is his own. With this plot device, the derailing is complete and the emotional economy firmly in place: the Indian labourers fight each other leaving the racialised colonial plantation system intact.

The novel concludes with a quick reconciliation scene between Lutchmee and Dilloo in the local Obeah man's jungle camp presenting this emotional economy as if in a nutshell. Nastily racist, the narrator describes the "obe man" as "an African of the lowest type" with "baboon-like features" which "altogether made a creature whose physical characteristics were worthy of the terror inspired by his infernal profession" (Jenkins 353). Thus, the Obeah man functions as the very incarnation of the white owners' fear (Jenkins 229, 349) of "insurrection" (348) that continues to haunt the plantation economy after emancipation. This fear had earlier put them into "rage" (227), "passionate excitement" (257, 262), "angry excitement" (258) and finally the very "terror" (289) that the narrator now ascribes to the Obeah man. His equipment inspires "grotesque horror" (355), a hyperbolic description preparing the melodramatic dying scene, which comes with a slightly comic edge, though.

This time the butt of the comedy are not the African characters[6] but the white reverend who offers Dilloo conversion to Christianity. With a final instant of derailing anger by directing its cognition of resentment at religion instead of humiliating exploitation, the novel renders Dilloo's last words in Pidgin English. Tellingly, it reserves the correct standard usage of the genitive for his oppressors: "'No!' cried the dying Coolie, loudly, almost fiercely, and with unconscious but terribly pointed satire [...] 'No! No! Jesu Kriss Massa Drummond's God – Massa Marston's God – all Inglees God. No God for Coolie!'" (358) Drummond and Marston, the head manager on Dilloo's estate and the local magistrate, stand out as the embodied material objects of Dilloo's anger. However, the only successful resistance the novel allows its dying protagonist is to reject the caricature of a clergyman on a civilising mission.

The immaterial objects of his anger are the exploitative economic relations that leave Dilloo and his fellow workers at the mercy of those who dictate the conditions of their existence. This group comprises the government-paid Bengali recruiter in India, a set of white estate managers and overseers, white and mixed-race drivers and white colonial administrative staff in Guyana. Drummond, the allegedly "naturally kind-hearted" (66) head-manager, who is repeatedly designated as "planter" as if he owned the estate, cautions his Scottish apprentice manager Craig against relying on everyday racism acquired in the relations with the "dark races by whom his wealth was made for him" (66):

---

6   Employing an impressive array of sub-genres to racialise his characters, Jenkins assigns the lowest form of slap-stick comedy to black characters – a feature most contemporaneous reviewers mention as "native". F. D. Owen, reviewing the novel for The Academy uses a striking postpositive litotes to describe a feature that is quite common in colonial novels set in the Caribbean before and after abolition: "[Dialogue] is chiefly represented by a little negro foolery of the usual order, not at all unamusing, but merely episodic" (Owen 547).

"You will never do for Demerara, my fine fellow," said the planter. "These niggers are brought here to work, and you must make them do it by hook or by crook. With your squeamish views, they would soon get the whip-hand of us; and we might as well shut up shop altogether." (171)

Craig, however, does not wish to treat the contract labourers, whom the manager tellingly equates with (enslaved) Africans disciplined by the whip, as suggested by his superior. This is remarkable because earlier in the story Craig had been stabbed by a Chinese labourer while attempting to arrest him for murder – falsely, as the reader knows, because the culprit once again is Hunoomaun. Craig survives the attack nursed by Lutchmee, which gives him some insight into her and her husband's lives. While Drummond, the planter's deputy, appreciates Dilloo's capacities as an exceptionally able worker (66, 96-97) he nevertheless detests him as "the spokesperson for his brethren" and "a firebrand" (169), Craig entertains a more respectful view of him. Subsequently, the novel sets up Craig as the centre for the readers' identification, augmenting this function with the generic devices of romance. Craig's love interest, however, is not Lutchmee – as she would be in the tradition of plantation fiction, which surfaces in Drummond's Creole "housekeeper" (71) – but the fair daughter of the local stipendiary magistrate, a relationship the narrator handles with some satirical distance. The relationship between Lutchmee and Craig, however, he stages differently – and with a purpose. Focusing on the young Indian woman, the narrator suggestively states:

> The Coolie [Lutchmee] had hitherto been giving herself up to her genial toil, with a devotion which by degrees grew to an enthusiasm, as her intimacy with the manly young Briton increased. [...] The life was new. It brought into her life fresh human elements, feelings she had never experienced before: ideas – novel, sweet, piquant. [...] she could not analyse the meaning of the feeling [...]. (155)

Whereas David Dabydeen recognises here "a nascent feminism, a nascent defiance of patriarchal structures" (Dabydeen 18), I read the Craig-Lutchmee subplot as part of the novel's emotional economy which relies on derailing. The subplot redirects the discontent and anger arising from the racist plantation order in two ways: it provides another object for Dilloo's anger and rage and it constructs two lovable characters that emotionally appeal to the British metropolitan readers. When Craig shakes Lutchmee's hand in sincere gratitude, the narrator assures the reform-oriented among his readers that, at this moment, "the antipathy of race finally died within him; and [...] this woman, without reference to colour or features, became to him as a fellow-being of one blood and one humanity with himself" (Jenkins 156). With this, "the pretty animal" (130) that Craig saw in Lutchmee earlier changes from "a subject of anxiety" into "an object of sympathy" (259, also 264, 269). Later he benevolently accompanies her to her husband's deathbed even though this makes him complicit in the murder. With Craig, the novel channels the readers' empathy with the dying Indian and his soon-to-be-abandoned wife through the emotions of a white man whose shy love affair with the magistrate's daughter makes him all the more likeable. She shortly follows suit developing "an actual sympathy" for Lutchmee (263, also 269).

While Craig and his beloved serve as models for the readers, whom the novel calls upon to grow equally benevolent moral sentiments, the second function of the subplot is overtly political. To demand their rights, the contract labourers, led by rich Dilloo (184, 303) and a free Indian banker and money-lender (104), whom the narrator labels "The Conspirators" (chapter heading, 145), employ a white lawyer to petition the governor (222ff.). Dilloo tells his wife: "'We are engaged in a great plot. Coolies on every estate are pledged to it. At first we are going to act peaceably and demand justice from the great Sahib, the Governor. If he will not give it to us, then ---' he stopped [...]" (163). While the narrator, repeatedly arguing as if he was a lawyer (230, also 160, 199, 223), supports the Indians' claims, he shows in dramatic detail how their en-

tering into industrial dispute provokes the planters to such a "West Indian rage" (227) that they press the magistrate and the governor to reject
it. The Craig-Lutchmee subplot, however, serves to remove this legally
supported industrial action from the readers' attention focussing it, in
turn, on a private matter as an object of rage and anger:

> But how greatly had his frank, manly nature suffered from the scorching bars
> of unjust justice, and the withering influence of ungenerous treatment! His
> mind was diseased with the sense of wrong, suspicion, resentment, the crav-
> ing thirst for revenge, and he regarded the incidents of this meeting between
> his wife and the overseer with jealousy and anger. (303)

While the novel uses the tadja, a fictional blend of Muslim and Hindoo
procession with dancing and ritual mock battles (cf. Moore 219ff.), to
send Dilloo out to fight Hunoomaun, the daughter of the magistrate, influenced by Craig, takes her father to task for not having done his duty
by the labourers (194ff.). The text suspends the irony and mild satire it
generally uses for the white legal elite to introduce the moral change of
the magistrate who begins to resist verbally the close surveillance on the
part of the planters who press him to serve their interests (199). This is
the only critical thrust that the novel promotes: it calls for improved legal
regulations for contract labour, arguing that both sides benefit from such
diligent and reliable workers as Dilloo to realise their potential (160-61,
223, 230). To put this across, the text infuses its social realism with elements of the political and legal pamphlet, which annoyed the reviewer
of the *London Society* ("New Books" 565) and others. With the dominant realist narrative and its emotional economy of colonial capitalism,
however, the novel subverts its own rational argument. Yet, the emotional argument is most successful in silencing anger and rage, emotions
that threaten the plantation economy and its exploitation of cheap brown
labour. Instead, the novel's deep plot encourages the metropolitan middle-class readers to condescendingly feel sympathy for suffering working-class Indians and identify with loving and fortunately reforming
middle-class colonial whites.

CONCLUSION

My interpretation of this colonial novel written by a mid-19th-century white male uses the category of emotion to connect the conception of imagined economies with the antiracist activism of Reni Eddo-Lodge and Afua Hirsch by paying special attention to the objects and cognitions of anger as fostered by global capitalism.

With this, I suggest re-reading colonial fiction not primarily in service of today's identity politics which value it for the representation of neglected non-white ethnic groups. Instead, I propose the use of this text as one of a type to demonstrate the economic and emotional rationale of its aesthetics on the level of character, plot and sub-genres. The generic blend of social realism and legal pamphlet, of revenge tragedy and melodrama, of comedy and satire allows for a multi-layered argument that, despite its ambiguities, normalises the extensive exploitation of migrant labourers in the colonial plantation economy. To break up this normalising discourse, I propose to analyse these very ambiguities and internal contradictions as strategies of racialisation for plainly economic ends. As a result, the exploitation of cheap black and brown labour loses its alleged 'normality' and becomes visible as a condition for private profits of which the British (and Western) public has always had its share in being able to buy cheap goods, including novels.

To overcome the select epistemological silence and to make useful the equally select emotional eloquence on the connection between race and capitalist economy, literary studies scholars can benefit from the impressive work of Catherine Hall and her team of black and white historians. For more than a decade, they have researched the legacies of British slave-ownership and documented the results in numerous publications and on a website with a continuously expanding database.

> Slave-ownership is virtually invisible in British history. It has been elided by strategies of euphemism and evasion originally adopted by the slave-owners themselves and subsequently reproduced widely in British culture. [...]

Against this background, our project is to reinscribe slave-ownership onto modern British history." (Hall et al. 1-2)

In her tellingly titled essay "Gendering Property, Racing Capital", Catherine Hall adds an observation that ties in with Reni Eddo-Lodge: "Disavowal and distantiation have been crucial mechanisms facilitating avoidance and evasion [...]. Our focus on British slave-ownership is a way of bringing slavery home and problematizing whiteness as an identity that carried privilege and power [...]" (24-25). In this vein, literary studies should transform anger into a motivation to analyse how aesthetically constructed emotions mediate the connections between race and capitalism. These emotions always key into the economy – imagined and real.

REFERENCES

Clarke, John. "Imagined, Real and Moral Economies." *Culture Unbound*, vol. 6, 2014, pp. 95-112, www.cultureunbound.ep.liu.se/article.asp?DOI=10.3384/cu.2000.1525.14695.

Dabydeen, David. "Introduction." Edward Jenkins. *Lutchmee and Dilloo. A Study of West Indian Life*. 1877. Edited and with a new introduction by David Dabydeen, Caribbean Classics, Macmillan Education, 2003, pp. 1-21.

D'Aguiar, Fred. "Letter to Beryl Gilroy." *Callaloo*, vol. 39, no. 4, 2016, pp. 757-61.

—. "Against Black British Literature." *Tibisiri. Caribbean Writers and Critics*, edited by Maggie Butcher, Dangeroo Press, 1988, pp. 106-14.

Eddo-Lodge, Reni. *Why I'm No Longer Talking to White People about Race*. Bloomsbury Circus, 2017.

Frevert, Ute. "Introduction." *Moral Economies*, edited by Ute Frevert, Vandenhoeck & Ruprecht, 2019, pp. 7-12.

—. "Moral Economies, Present and Past. Social Practices and Intellectual Controversies." *Moral Economies*, edited by Ute Frevert, Vandenhoeck & Ruprecht, 2019, pp. 13-44.

Graves, R. P., and Lynn Milne. "John Edward Jenkins." *Oxford Dictionary of National Biography*, Oxford University Press, 2004. doi. org/10.1093/ref:odnb/34175. 31 July 2019.

Hall, Catherine. "Gendering Property, Racing Capital." *History Workshop Journal*, vol. 78, 2014, pp. 22-38.

—, Nicholas Draper, and Keith McClelland. "Introduction." *Legacies of British Slave-Ownership. Colonial Slavery and the Formation of Victorian Britain*, edited by Catherine Hall, Nicholas Draper, Keith McClelland, Katie Donington and Rachel Lang, Cambridge University Press, 2014, pp. 1-33.

Hirsch, Afua. *Brit(ish): On Race, Identity and Belonging*. Jonathan Cape, 2018.

Illouz, Eva. "Introduction: Emodities or the Making of Emotional Commodities." *Emotions as Commodities. Capitalism, Consumption and Authenticity*, edited by Eva Illouz, Routledge, 2018, pp. 1-29.

Jackson, Joseph. "Introduction." Edward Jenkins. *Lutchmee and Dilloo. A Study of West Indian Life*. 1877. Edited and introduced by Joseph Jackson, The Guyana Classics Library, The Caribbean Press for the Government of Guyana, 2010, pp. xi-xx.

Jagdeo, Bharrat President. "Series Preface." Edward Jenkins. *Lutchmee and Dilloo. A Study of West Indian Life*. 1877. Edited and introduced by Joseph Jackson, The Guyana Classics Library, The Caribbean Press for the Government of Guyana, 2010, pp. v-vi.

Jenkins, Edward. *Lutchmee and Dilloo. A Study of West Indian Life*. 1877. Edited and with a new introduction by David Dabydeen, Caribbean Classics, Macmillan Education, 2003.

—. *Ginx's Baby. His Birth and Other Misfortunes*. 1871. Henry King & Co., 1873.

—. *Little Hodge*. Henry King & Co., 1872.

Klein, Alison. *Anglophone Literature of Caribbean Indenture: The Seductive Hierarchies of Empire*. Palgrave Macmillan, 2018.

Legacies of British Slave-Ownership. http://www.ucl.ac.uk/lbs/.

Leong, Nancy. "Racial Capitalism." *Harvard Law Review*, vol. 126, no. 8, 2013, pp. 2153-226.

"Literature." *Lloyd's Weekly Newspaper*, 28 October 1977, issue 1823, p. 5. *British Library Newspapers, Part One: 1800-1900*.

"Literature: Novels of the Week." *The Athenaeum*, 20 October 1877, issue 2608, pp. 491-92.

"London Correspondence." *Western Mail*, 19 October 1877, issue 2641, p. 2. *British Library Newspapers, Part One: 1800-1900*.

"Lutchmee and Dilloo." *Saturday Review of Politics, Literature, Science and Art*, 8 December 1877, vol. 44, issue 1154, pp. 719-20.

Moore, Brian L. *Cultural Power, Resistance and Pluralism. Colonial Guyana, 1838-1900*. Press of the University of the West Indies and McGill Queen's University Press, 1995.

"New Books." *London Society: An Illustrated Magazine of Light and Amusing Literature for the Hours of Relaxation*, December 1877, vol. 32, no. 192, pp. 554-70.

Owen, F. M. "New Novels." *The Academy*, 15 December 1877, issue 293, pp. 547-48.

Poynting, Jeremy. "John Edward Jenkins and the Imperial Conscience." *The Journal of Commonwealth Literature*, vol. 21, no. 1, 1986, pp. 211-21.

Rejlander, Oscar Gustav. "Ginx's Baby." *Royal Photographic Society Collection*, collections.vam.ac.uk/item/O1394739/ginxs-baby-photograph-rejlander-oscar-gustav/.

Smith, Jonathan. *Charles Darwin and Victorian Visual Culture*. Cambridge University Press, 2006.

Sutherland, John. *The Stanford Companion to Victorian Fiction*. Stanford University Press, 1989.

Thompson, Edward P. "The Moral Economy of the English Crowd in the Eighteenth Century." *Past and Present*, vol. 50, 1971, pp. 76-136.

Ulich, Dieter, and Philipp Mayring. *Psychologie der Emotionen*. Kohlhammer, 1992.

Woodmansee, Martha, and Mark Osteen. "Taking Account of the New Economic Criticism: an Historical Introduction." *The New Economic Criticism. Studies at the Intersection of Literature and Economics*, edited by Martha Woodmansee and Mark Osteen, Routledge, 1999, pp. 3-50.

Imagining Money

Jason G. Allen

INTRODUCTION

John Clarke presents the theme of this volume by asking why we might speak of "imagined economies". It is, he answers, "to interrupt the apparent ubiquity of economies", to provide a moment for "a pause for thought". In this chapter, I explore the role that imagination plays in the creation and maintenance of a money system. Money is important to the existence and functioning of an economy.[1] Money, too, seems ubiquitous and naturally-occurring, so I want to pause and consider why it is that we might have money and what exactly it is doing. Different objects have served as money, or tokens of money, in different societies. Today, the main form of money (from an economic perspective, if not from a

---

1 Granted, non-monetary economies exist, and it is a worthwhile project to imagine economies that function without money (as we know it, or at all). And granted, money plays a lesser role in the lived experience of numerous communities, especially in the Global South, where traditional webs of social obligation still operate in parallel to the money-based economy. And granted further, important categories of economic activity subsist even in money-based economies (for example in the domestic sphere). But money is central to the type of (financial capitalist) economy with which many chapters in this collection are concerned.

strictly legal one) is digital representations of credit-debt relations between a person and a commercial bank. In other times and places, money
has taken the form of, or been represented by, scrips of paper, metal
discs, shells, and various consumable and non-consumable commodities. But what is *money itself*, and where does it come from?

In this chapter, I draw on the concepts of social ontology and make
some reflections on the role of law and legal systems in constituting
money. Money, like so much of our social world, is successful because
it appears natural and self-evident; but it is fundamentally mind-dependent, which is to say that it only exists because a community of people
think it does. In a meaningful sense, it is "imagined". This provides the
opportunity to bring to the volume another tradition of thinking about
"real fictions" in the analytical idiom typical of English and Scandina-
vian legal philosophy, and to explore the role of "imagination" in the
constitution of a money system.

MONEY IN MACROECONOMICS

The first observation to be made is that, if we want to get to the bottom
of money, it is not (only) to economics as a discipline that we should
turn. It is perhaps startling for non-economists that the dominant school
of macroeconomic thought has no place for money as such. "Dynamic
stochastic general equilibrium" models posit that, given certain assumptions, there exists a set of prices for every commodity in an economy in
general equilibrium (Rogers). In effect, the better an economy works,
the less conceptual need it has of money. Thus, Frank Hahn observed in
1983:

> The most serious challenge that the existence of money poses to the theorist
> is this: the best developed model of the economy cannot find room for it. The
> best developed model is, of course, the Arrow-Debreu version of Walrasian
> general equilibrium. A world in which all contingent future contracts are
> possible neither needs nor wants intrinsically worthless money. A first, and

to a fastidious theorist difficult, task is to find an alternative construction without thereby sacrificing the clarity and logical coherence that are such outstanding features of Arrow-Debreu. (Hahn 1)[2]

Since the Global Financial Crisis ("GFC") of 2008, more heterodox economists have stressed the importance of making conceptual room for the existence of money in macroeconomic modelling (for example, Goodhart et al.). In large part, this requires integration of the *financial system* into macroeconomic models, reflecting the role that financial intermediaries, particularly banks, play in money-creation. The best accounts of "modern money" explain that banks do not just accept deposits of pre-existing, real resources and then lend them to borrowers; banks create money *ex nihilo*, as it were, by lending (Jakab and Kumhof). The traditional arrangement forms a kind of "finance franchise" between (private) licensed commercial banks and the (public) central bank, in which the former play a systemic role (Hockett and Omarova). Currently, non-bank financial intermediaries (especially payments services providers) are, in turn, encroaching on that traditional role, making accurate theory more important than ever (Omarova).

Meanwhile, classical economists since the 1970s have been concerned to build macroeconomic models on stable "micro" foundations, including actor preferences, responses regulation, technology, and resource constraints (Lucas). But their micro-foundations have not always been very accurate depictions of the complex social reality of the empirical economy (Lawson, *Economics* 21; Hodge 182). And a distinctly legal perspective is needed here; as Katharina Pistor has argued, law and finance are locked in a dynamic relationship in which new forms of contractual behaviour challenge existing legal rules but seek, in turn, legal vindication; this means that the legal structure of finance is critical to explaining the behaviour of market participants (Pistor). It is essential,

---

2   For a critique of Hahn's efforts to find an alternative construction, see Hyman Minsky.

then, not only to include money in macroeconomic models of the economy, but also to ensure that we have the best account of the nature of
money itself.

Both these points underline the need for a complex ontology of
money, based in complex social practices. And they both suggest a role
for law and therefore legal theory in explaining what money is and how
it is made.

There are various ways in which one could construct a taxonomy of
monetary theories: one reads of metallist *versus* non-metallist theories,
realist *versus* nominalist, commodity *versus* credit, orthodox *versus* heterodox, endogenous *versus* exogenous, currency *versus* banking, so on
and so forth. There are important correlations between these various dichotomies, and many of them cut across each other, as well.[3] All imply
a set of ontological and metaphysical commitments. Theorists often
speak at cross purposes across these dichotomies, not least because they
keep those metaphysical and ontological commitments tacit rather than
articulating them. It is beyond my ambition to explore the taxonomy of
monetary theories here. I wish to use just one way of contrasting approaches to the concept of money – what I will call *market theories of
money* and *legal theories of money*.[4] In the former, "money" is created
through the transactional activities of market participants, typically said
to evolve from primitive barter through the (spontaneous, or at least mar-
ket-driven) emergence of one commodity (typically a precious metal) as
a medium of exchange. In the latter, money is posited as the creature of
legal convention, typically said to derive from the interventions of an
organised political authority.

---

3   Joseph Schumpeter's summa divisio was between commodity and credit the-
    ories (Schumpeter 649).
4   Actually, the law plays a constitutive role in both, as it is in virtue of the legal
    system that we have the prerequisites of a market – i.e. (private) property
    rights that can be transferred by contract. Without these two legal construc-
    tions, we would have nothing like a "market" in the modern sense at all.

In their starker forms, these approaches are mutually exclusive. Indeed, the nature of money was one of the focal points of the *Methodenstreit* between the Austrian School and the German Historical School. Carl Menger, for the former, argued for a commodity-based market theory of money. According to this view, money has to be understood as the "spontaneous outcome, the unpremeditated resultant, of particular, individual efforts of the members of a society, who have little by little worked their way to a discrimination of the different degrees of saleableness in commodities" (Menger 250). Georg Knapp, for the latter, presented the "State Theory of Money", arguing that "[m]oney is a creature of law" and that it was a mistake to equate "money" with metal coins; "money, whether of metal or paper, is only a special case of a means of payment in general", and this means of payment arises in a society when the state stipulates that taxes will be accepted in a certain token, giving that token value for individuals transacting *inter se* (Knapp 2).

Both these approaches trace right back to the beginning of the Western tradition of theorising about money – Aristotle here emphasising money as a creature of convention, and there emphasising the metallic nature of money in the ancient world.[5] Both have obvious merit. The Austrian School usefully points to the role of individual choices in the creation of a money system, and, despite an element of "just so" theorising about the vagaries of barter, presents a credible attempt to understand the metaphysics of money in the Aristotelian tradition (Smith). The German Historical School view, on the other hand, seems better supported by the archaeological and historical evidence on the evolution of money and barter (Ingham 47, 211), affords a greater conceptual role for networks of credit and debt that historically operated alongside coin-based money systems, and does a better job of explaining the forms of

---

5   Aristotle, Nichomachean Ethics 156, "this is why we call it νόμισμα, because its value is derived, not from nature but from law [νόμος] and can be altered or abolished at will." Cf Aristotle, Politics 42.

money that have predominated for the past century (quite possibly much longer) (Desan 25).

Knapp's approach has become the foundation of what I regard as the more credible schools of monetary theory in modern times. The crux of Knapp's view of money appears in his assertion that even full-bodied coins are "chartal", i.e. that their nominal face value provides the "money" element, not the metal. Without special agreement between the parties, a debt could not be discharged by the delivery of a quantum of metal; where such an agreement is general, indeed universal, the "moneyness" of the coin is a matter of law and custom, not its physical properties (Olivecrona 47-48). Thus Knapp put the metaphysics of the complex institutional landscape which underpins money's existence – complex credit and debt relationships involving not only individuals but also the "state" – into the centre of theoretical efforts.[6] In my view, this provides a more credible answer to the question Menger himself posed, i.e. why economic agents are so willing to exchange their goods for "little metal disks apparently useless as such, or for documents representing [them]" (Menger 239).[7]

However, Knapp's view perhaps puts too little emphasis on the role of private transactional behaviour in creating money systems. And it focusses perhaps too much on the state, and on law as a creature of the state, giving too little attention to private payment communities and their customary norms (Hodgson 331). Further, Knapp's account itself exhausts itself precisely where it ought to explain the nature of the mone-

6   H.S. Ellis credited Knapp with bringing the metaphysical questions concerning money to the foreground in a manner "unparalleled in the history of economics" (Ellis vii).

7   Georg Simmel rightly noted: "[M]etallic money is also a promise to pay and ... it differs from the cheque only with respect to the size of the group which vouches for its being accepted" (174-79). In a similar vein, J.M. Keynes observed that the Indian Rupee "being a token coin, [was] virtually a note printed on silver" (26).

tary unit; while he succeeds in explaining the physical media of payment, he fails, because of his historical method of reference back to "autometallism", to explain the nominalist unit of value itself (the dollar, euro, or pound sterling) as an object in its own right (Olivecrona 99). In systems such as our own in which there is no reserve of commodities to which the monetary unit refers, we must be concerned with this purely nominalistic unit first and foremost. As Karl Olivecrona observed in 1953, individuals and private (commercial) banks can issue more "IOUs" than they can pay; when a central bank, on the other hand, is not compelled to honour its debts (e.g. by selling gold on foreign exchanges), its solvency is perfect: "Paradoxically enough the claims on the central bank are always good because they can never be honoured. Payment does not come into question, since there are no media of payment available" (Olivecrona 63). This creates a debt situation of a particular kind, which we are only now beginning properly to theorise (e.g. McLeay et al.). So-called "Modern Monetary Theory" has been moving inwards from the periphery of monetary theory, and has recently been receiving attention even from central bankers (e.g. Weber).

I will leave this discussion here, however, for it is to the theoretical presuppositions of both major schools that I wish to turn. In effect, I wish to argue that they both require something in the nature of a "real fiction". Karl Elster (an acolyte of Knapp) argued in a 1920 essay on the "purchasing power" and "validity" of money:

[Money] is not a commodity, even where it has surely arisen from a commodity. Money arises – arises from a commodity – by way of an *individual-psychological process*. A good does not become money through being ever more greatly valued, it arises rather because the reason for its valuation changes fundamentally; a good does not become money in virtue of being the most valued commodity, but because it ceases to be a commodity. Die and become! Money is created in the same instant in which the good ends its conceptual existence. (247; emphasis added)

This seems to grasp something fundamental about the nature of money – that a thing, whatever it is, assumes a monetary status *in virtue of being treated as such by individuals within a community*. Commodity theories of money, especially, distract us with the notion that the money-token has "intrinsic worth", being made of a precious metal. Elster makes clear that as soon as a piece of gold is used as money (rather than as a necklace or as bullion, or as an electrical conductor for that matter) its *natural properties* fade into the conceptual background. Likewise, if I take a gold coin and turn it into an ornament, or use it as a paperweight, or to bodge a blown fuse in my car, I wrench it from the monetary domain back into the domain of commodities – I stop treating it as if it embodied an abstract, intangible monetary unit, and start using it for its physical properties (shininess, weight, conductivity).

Something similar can be said of the liabilities that circulate as money in a modern monetary system. They only work because they pass around as currency – because they provide a standard unit of measuring value. If we were to fix quanta of "book money" into place as bi-lateral obligations between two certain, identified parties, their monetary status would vanish. This is reflected in the English law of financial instruments; originally, things like debt writings could not circulate as a token of payment because they were legal obligations that could only be transferred through a difficult process called "novation" in which the parties agreed that a new party could enter the relationship to replace the old one. It was only over time that the financial instruments we know today as "negotiable" were recognised to pass "in currency" and therefore to play a role that assimilated coin (e.g. Holdsworth 997). Again, modern developments including "cryptocurrencies" are challenging settled notions, for example in the question whether a bitcoin is capable of being owned and whether ownership can pass with change of "possession".[8]

Christine Desan rightly argues that this brings the *monetary unit* into the foreground of our theoretical focus:

---

8   The problem is that possession, as traditionally understood, is impossible in the case of an intangible object like a bitcoin (Allen).

Money is neither an object – the lump of silver that the philosopher imagined, nor an abstraction – the convention that those observing paper money
assume. Money is, instead, a *method of representing and moving resources
within a group*: it is a way of referencing or entailing material value that
creates a unit to measure other resources over time, pay off obligations finally, and transfer value immediately. (Desan 21; emphasis added)

As her examples show, we can use various things to achieve this method,
i.e. to represent the monetary unit. And much of the scholarship on the
nature of money is focussed squarely on the money token, not this monetary unit. This focus has, in turn, informed the background against
which much of our law has evolved, and explains the common inability
to look past the brute object that serves as a token of the monetary unit
(see Appleby 43).

Shifting our focus helps to reveal that money (whatever it is, and
whatever is used for it) has a social ontology. My intuition is that, as
Tony Lawson has argued, engagement with the social ontology of
money may in fact reconcile some of the points of disagreement between
the great schools of monetary theory, showing them to be theories about
different *historical instances* of money rather than about the *ontological
nature* of money itself (Lawson, "Social Positioning" 961-62). In my
view, an enquiry into the latter would, however, appear to be an enquiry
into the nature of an object – albeit a quasi-abstract or "imaginary" one
that is defined by its function as an economic coordination mechanism
(Smit et al. 327). But this is a point on which reasonable minds differ –
just as it served as a major clashpoint in the *Methodenstreit*, there is a
live debate within the emerging field of social ontology on precisely this
question: Is "money" a *token* of something, or the something for which
there is a token. [9]

---

9   I thank Tony Lawson for this formulation in his comments on the draft.

REAL FICTIONS

The editors have discussed Günther Teubner's notion of the *"Real-fiktion"*. Another branch of theory that deals with the reality of apparently fictional objects is social ontology, a branch of analytical metaphysics concerned with the existence of socially constructed artefacts. Social ontologists have indeed thought and written much on money, and their efforts can help us, in turn, to understand the role of "imagination" in the creation of a money-based economy. As Uskali Mäki observes, in a discussion of the methodology of economics, social ontology has much to say about that discipline's foundations:

> Economics deals with preferences and expectations, strategies and interactions, demand and supply, trust and fairness, laws and conventions, agents and principals, and markets and governments. One can try to construe these items without invoking anything mental or social, but yet it seems obvious that whatever those terms are taken to refer to *does not exist mind-independently* and, therefore, are not in the same category with electrons, cells, continents and galaxies. (7; emphasis added)

Of the many stories that could be told of money's development over time, one story that has particular resonance today is that of *dematerialisation*. It is important not to stress the linearity of this trend, because much of the history of money has over-emphasised the role of coin. The amount of coin circulating in medieval European economies, for example, has been demonstrated to be much smaller than the economies themselves – the rest ran on complex webs of credit and debt (Gleeson ch. 3, "Money and Credit", for a discussion and references). Tally debts are at least 2,000 years older than the oldest coins, and account-based money systems have been more common throughout history ancient and modern than the textbooks generally recognise (Wray 45). So a straightforward story of "metal to paper to digital money" would seriously mischaracterise the actual course of development.

But there is something to be said for exploring the theme of demate-rialisation over the past century, as we have seen the concept and the practice of money loose itself from precious metal, and then from cash (in the form of banknotes and non-precious metal coins) as digital infor-mation systems were used to record and transfer value. Olivecrona ob-served, somewhat presciently, in 1957:

> Theoretically, all payments could be carried out without the use of cash. Book money could, indeed, be made the sole medium of payment. Every-body would then receive his income in the form of drafts on a bank and pay for his expenses in the same way. But this would be so cumbersome as to be hardly feasible. Cash money is needed besides book money for two reasons: (i) to facilitate small payments, and (ii) to make possible instant payment by unknown persons and other persons who are not entrusted with credit. (58)

It should be apparent that both of Olivecrona's impediments have been removed by advances in information technology since he wrote. Ironi-cally, today cash constitutes less than 2% of Olivecrona's native econ-omy, and Sweden is leading the way in cashless payment systems in-cluding proposals for an "e-Krona" issued by the Sverige Riksbank ("E-krona").

Counterintuitively, dematerialisation helps us to see what I perceive to be the essential properties of money more clearly. I will demonstrate how this is the case by presenting a brief overview of some of the efforts made by social ontologists to describe the ontology of money.

John Searle's 1995 book presents the basic formula for his account of the construction of social reality: an institutional fact (e.g. a marriage, a president, or a dollar) is created when a community takes a brute fact (i.e. an act, object, or event) to "count as" an institutional fact in a certain context.[10] An institutional fact is essentially a bundle of deontic powers (i.e. rights, duties, prohibitions, etc.) that give agents desire-independent reasons for action. For example, when a wooden figurine becomes a "rook", it starts doing new things within the context of a game of chess, such as "castling" or putting a "king" into the status of "check". Searle describes the logico-linguistic operation involved in transforming a figurine into a rook as "X counts as Y in C" where X is the brute object (wooden figurine), Y is the institutional object composed of deontic powers (the rook with its capacities to move and attack) and C is the context (a game of chess).

For Searle, there are two types of social fact (Brey 70; Searle, *The Construction*; Searle, *Making the Social*). Both relate to the brute objects and events in different ways. First are ordinary social facts, such as that this four-legged object is a "chair" or that this sharp object is a "knife". Social facts come into existence when a community of people impose a function on an object that is inherently capable of performing the function – it has properties such as stability or sharpness. Second are institutional facts. These come into existence when a community imposes a function on an object that is not inherently capable to perform that function in virtue of its physical properties alone. Unlike being a chair, for example, which involves supporting a human in a sitting position, being a "throne" does not depend on a physical property of an object as such (although thrones are often decorated as a reflection of their ritual status). The essential properties of "throne-ness" exist only in human minds – i.e. in shared intentional states and perceptions (Johansson 74).

In Searle's scheme, money is an institutional fact par excellence. Searle's formula is, predictably, the subject of a number of disputes among social ontologists. First, there is a long-standing dispute with Tony Lawson, which is also of interest as a showcase for the differences

---

10 E.g. that I am married, that we have a contract, that tomorrow is Thursday, that the Soviet Union no longer exists. The basic distinction between institutional facts and brute facts is explained in G.E.M. Anscome (69) (generally see Searle, The Construction).

of approach between the Cambridge and Berkeley schools of social ontology. Where Searle seems to stipulate that the X term of a status function like "money" must not be capable of performing the relevant function in virtue of its physical properties alone, Lawson insists that in order to be "positioned" as money within a "totality", the thing positioned must possess properties that make it capable of being money:

> Social positioning is the term for the process whereby, through general acceptance throughout a community, human individuals, things or other phenomena become incorporated as components of these emergent totalities. In all cases, social positioning involves the generalised acceptance of the following three elements in regards to any item that is thereby positioned: 1) the allocation of an agreed status, 2) its practical placement as a component of a totality, and 3) the harnessing of certain of its capacities already possessed to serve as one or more system functions of the totality. ("Social Positioning" 964)

For Lawson, there is (i) a position, (ii) the occupant of a position (*qua* brute fact), (iii) the *positioned* occupant, and (iv) the *token* of the positioned occupant. For Lawson, the essential definition of money relates to (iii), whatever (ii) might be. Lawson might argue that the money-token, in order to be positioned as (occupy the social position of) "money", must be durable, unique, and non-forgeable ("Social Positioning" 968). Although I would confess Searleian tendencies, I think Lawson must be right that the thing positioned as money must have some basic properties. Beans make better counters than bananas because they are more durable. Gold makes better counters than beans because it is scarcer. Cigarettes make better counters than water because they are more readily individualised. Taking this point, I will leave the Searle/Lawson debate for now, because I think that the water example provides a good impulse to the next point, which relates to the *quasi-abstract mathematical units* that appear in any money system. Suffice it to say that for both Lawson and Searle, despite their methodological differences, the establishment of a given social position, and the allocation of people or objects to it, is ultimately a matter of community acceptance. This keeps the story of money squarely in the realm of mind-dependent phenomena.

The debate within social ontology is highly relevant to the changes we are now witnessing with payments technology, too, although it is fair to say that a great number of questions remain to be answered. Following Searle's 1995 statement of his basic formula, Barry Smith observed that some institutional facts, such as electronic money, do not have a physical X term at all. In place of metal and paper, electronic book-money (for example) rests on digital information structures that are poorly captured by the basic formula. Smith asserted that these were in fact free-standing Y terms, i.e. institutional facts (bundles of deontic powers) not resting on a brute fact. Searle responded by introducing a variation to his theory; he accepted the existence of Y terms for which there is no X term, and said that the logico-linguistic operation involved is simply a declaration that "Y exists in C" (Barry and Searle 285). We need not get bogged down in the finer details of the debate, but Ingvar Johansson has rightly observed that no one has yet fully teased out the differences between the basic case of institutional facts anchored in a physical object and (apparently) free-standing institutional facts.

Johansson extends a classical analogy between money and chess, which offers some final impulses. A basic game of chess is played on a board with physical pieces. The transformation from a wooden figurine to a rook is explained by Searle's basic formula: "X (a wooden figure) counts as Y (a rook) in the context C (the game of chess)". This formula expresses the imposition of a function on a brute object: When we accept that a figurine counts as a rook, it starts doing things (in the context of a game of chess) that a wooden figurine could not. The status moves the natural object into a new domain of social reality. Johansson calls this basic case real chess.

Chess players often record their games, however, and for this purpose translate the chess pieces and board into an algebraic system of notation. Our rook is no longer a figurine but the letter "R"; the playspace is no longer a board but a column of notations on a set of Cartesian coordinates (e.g. R moves a1 to d1). In other words, the objects and events that constitute a game of chess are represented in documentary form. We can thus review particular games of chess as discrete, documented historical facts. Searle's basic formula no longer works in this context, however, as there is no X term. Johansson suggests that we instead use the formula "Z (our notation for rook) counts in C (a game of chess) as a representation of the basic formula (X (wooden figurine) counts as Y (a rook))". In this case we have an algebraic representation of a real game of chess. But the act of recording real chess using such notation opens up a further possibility, too. Imagine that we live in different cities. We send each other messages such as "R moves a1 to d1". We have now started playing a new form of chess, which Johansson calls account chess.

The interesting thing is that the objects and events that make up a game of account chess are particulars, rather than universals, but are neither straightforward spatio-temporal nor Platonic objects. Account chess is, according to Johansson, a fictional object. Intuitively, whatever else is said about the true ontological status of fictional objects, "we often speak and act as if there were such enduring, identifiable, and re-identifiable fictional particulars" (78-79). But even social ontologists have failed to present a persuasive framework for describing fictional social objects. To fill the gap, Johansson presents a scheme of fictional institutional facts, representational institutional facts, and primitive institutional facts (95).

Johansson then applies his scheme to the evolution of money. A traditional bank book that records movements of coins and banknotes is, like an algebraic documentation of a game of real chess, a representation of something else. But, like the algebraic chess notation, it bears the possibility of a new kind of money that exists only in information:

> Instead of material money transactions (compare: material chess moves) we now often have transactions by means of mere accounts of money (compare: moves in account chess). The latter kind of transaction is made in terms of a very special kind of fictional object, *account money*. What since long is

called "deposit money" and "checking account money" can be regarded as a species of account money. Such money can exist by means of both book-entries and computer databases. (Johansson 86)

This resonates, in broad terms at least, with a view recently put forward by J.P. Smit, Filip Buekens, and Stan du Plessis. A money system, they argue, is a set of positions on a relative ratio scale (342). The moving balance of this ratio is complex, with variables at the supply end as well as constant shifting in the position of money-users. The thing to remember is that coins and banknotes are only "money" because they are records of these positions. The token solves a practical problem of record-keeping, but it does not solve the basic problem of providing an object or tool of economic coordination. The existence of a monetary unit facilitates economic interactions, for example as captured by the classical functions of money as a unit of account, store of value, medium of exchange, and standard of deferred payment. The object of coordination is the monetary unit itself. Those units might be counted with the aid of metal disc, chits of paper, or digital records without any difference at the level of logical structure. That is, I think, the case with Johansson's "account money".

CONCLUSION

Whatever else money is, and whatever other elements are involved in its ontology, there is a substantial element of psychological disposition, which I think is aptly caught by the term "imagination". That is not to say that other psychological dispositions, such as trust or motivation, are not important to the creation and effective maintenance of a monetary system. But imagination is key; my trust, for example, is trust in the fact that certain objects represent positions on an imagined set of relations, denominated in an ideal unit. Perhaps the "essence" or "spirit" of money is a fiction. Money is a collective delusion, as it were, that is extremely helpful and effective in structuring certain types of social interactions, including economic transactions. In theorising this fiction, I hope that I have provided some points of interest at which social ontology, law, and economics might interact and cross-pollinate in future research.

I have not delved into the questions of politics and political economy that naturally arise around money. But I would like to conclude with three brief observations. First, once we recognise money as a creature of our own imagination, that owes a large part of its existence to that do-main of social reality we call "law" – rather than as a naturally-existing entity – it becomes difficult to deny a constitutional aspect to any mon-etary system. This appears most strongly in state theories of money, which identify money most closely with the organised political commu-nity. One may reject the notion that "money" is only possible in a mod-ern, Westphalian state, and point to other forms of political association with autonomous payment communities. But that does not negate the essential connection between politics, law, and money. This is an onto-logical argument about money in general, rather than a policy argument about the best kind of money system. Money is not a neutral fact of the universe to which human societies must conform, like the number of hours in the day or molecules of H_2O in a litre of water (Fox et al. 17). Money is a creature of social convention that serves certain purposes.

Secondly, this being the case, in my view money should function conformably with the constitutional values and aspirations of the rele-vant society. Where a money system ceases to do so, or systemically creates outcomes unconformable with those values, there is a *prima fa-cie* case to change it. This impulse is implicit in the "cryptocurrency" movement, which is seeking radically to reform the way that money is made. It seeks expressly to replace the need for both commercial banks and central banks – to circumvent the "finance franchise" entirely (Nakamoto). Given the timing of Bitcoin's launch, it is likely that its initiators wanted to provide a means to avoid outcomes such as central bank manipulation of the money supply through unconventional mone-tary operations like "quantitative easing" in the wake of the GFC. Or, put differently, to provide a means to undermine central bank monetary policy. Indeed, others perceive central bank control over the supply of money as an essential tool to promote monetary policy.

Thirdly, technologies, including the "blockchain" technology launched together with Bitcoin in 2009, offer new tools and affordances for both private and public actors to create money. For example, Rohan Grey has recently argued that central banks should embrace the opportunity to issue their own liabilities directly to the public on a much broader scale than ever before, in digital form as "central bank digital currency" ("CBDC"). While one of the chief risks associated with CBDC is a flight from commercial banks, Grey argues that this could catalyse a healthy re-alignment within the monetary system, in which commercial banks lose their monopoly on payments processing and focus on credit analysis and collateral evaluation (170-171). A number of central banks have explored options for CBDC, and some even have trials in progress (Gnan and Mascriando). The proposal in mid-2019 by Facebook and a consortium to launch "Libra", a digital currency backed by reserves of sovereign fiat currencies, may accelerate the time-line for these developments ("An Introduction to Libra"; Jones).

There has probably never been a more exciting time in the long history of money. It is difficult to predict what the long-term impacts of the last decade's developments will be, but it is safe to say that the monetary system will change fundamentally in the next ten years. Perhaps the crucial virtue in anyone thinking about the future of money at the present time would be imagination – the courage to take a moment, to reject the inevitability of legacy conventions, and to imagine what might be possible in the future.

REFERENCES

Allen, Jason G. "Negotiability in Digital Environments." *Butterworths Journal of International Banking and Finance Law*, vol. 34, no. 7, 2019, pp. 459-63.

"An Introduction to Libra." *Libra*, 18 July 2019, libra.org/en-US/wp-content/uploads/sites/23/2019/06/LibraWhitePaper_en_US.pdf.

Anscome, Gertrude E. M. "On Brute Facts." *Analysis*, vol.18, no. 3, 1958, pp. 69-72.

Appleby, Joyce O. "Locke, Liberalism, and the Natural Law of Money." *Past and Present,* vol. 71, 1976, pp. 43-69.

Aristotle. *Politics.* Translated by Benjamin Jowett, Clarendon Press, 1920.

—. *Nichomachean Ethics.* Translated by F. H. Peters, 5th ed., Kegan Paul, Trench, Truebner & Co, 1893.

Brey, Philip. "The Social Ontology of Virtual Objects." *American Journal of Economics and Sociology*, vol. 62, no. 1, 2003, pp. 269-82.

Desan, Christine. *Making Money.* Oxford University Press, 2014.

"E-krona." *Sveriges Riksbank,* 2019, www.riksbank.se/en-gb/payments--cash/e-krona/.

Ellis, Howard S. *German Monetary Theory 1905-1933.* Harvard University Press, 1934.

Elster, Karl. "'Kaufkraft' und 'Geltung' des Geldes." *Jahrbücher für Nationalökonomie und Statistik*, vol. 115, no. 1, 1920, pp. 243-49.

Fox, David, François R. Velde, and Wolfgang Ernst. "Monetary History Between Law and Economics." *Money in the Western Legal Tradition: Middle Ages to Bretton Woods*, edited by David Fox and Wolfgang Ernst, Oxford University Press, 2016, pp. 3-17.

Gleeson, Simon. *The Legal Concept of Money.* Oxford University Press, 2019.

Gnan, Ernest, and Donato Masciandro, editors. *Do We Need Central Bank Digital Currency? Economics, Technology and Institutions.* SUERF Conference Proceedings, 2018/2, www.suerf.org/docx/s_cf0d02ec99e61a64137b8a2c3b03e030_7025_suerf.pdf.

Goodhart, Charles A. E., Nikolas Romanidis, Dimitrios P. Tsomocos, and Martin Shubik. "Macro-Modelling, Default and Money." Saïd Business School WP, June 2016.

Grey, Rohan. "Banking in a Digital Fiat Currency Regime." *Regulating Blockchain: Techno-Social and Legal Challenges*, edited by Philipp Hacker, Ioannis Lianos, Georgios Dimitropoulos, and Stefan Eich, Oxford University Press, 2019.

Hahn, Frank. *Money and Inflation.* MIT Press, 1983.

Hockett, Robert, and Saule T. Omarova. "The Finance Franchise." *Cornell Law Review*, vol. 102, 2017, pp. 1143-218.

Hodge, Duncan. "Economics, Realism and Reality: A Comparison of Mäki and Lawson." *Cambridge Journal of Economics*, vol. 32, no. 2, 2008, pp. 163-202.

Hodgson, Geoffrey M. "Observations on the Legal Theory of Finance." *Journal of Comparative Economics,* vol. 41, no. 2, 2013, pp. 331-37.

Holdsworth, William S. "The History of the Treatment of 'Choses' in Action by the Common Law." *Harvard Law Review*, vol. 33, no. 8, 1920, pp. 997-1030.

Ingham, Geoffrey. *The Nature of Money.* Polity, 2004.

Jakab, Zoltan, and Michael Kumhof. "Banks are not intermediaries of loanable funds – and why this matters." Bank of England, Working Paper No. 529, 29 May 2015.

Johansson, Ingvar. "Money and Fictions." *Kapten Nemos Kolumbarium*, edited by Felix Larsson, Göteborg University, 2005, pp. 73-101.

Jones, Claire. "Central bank plans to create digital currencies receive backing." *Financial Times*, 30 June 2019, www.ft.com/content/428a0b20-99b0-11e9-9573-ee5cbb98ed36.

Keynes, John M. *The Collected Writings of John Maynard Keynes, Volume 1: Indian Currency and Finance.* Edited by Elizabeth Johnson and Donald Moggridge, Cambridge University Press, 1978.

Knapp, Georg. *The State Theory of Money.* Macmillan, 1924.

Lawson, Tony. *Economics and Reality.* Routledge, 1997.

—. "Social Positioning and the Nature of Money." *Cambridge Journal of Economics*, vol. 40, no. 4, 2016, pp. 961-96.

Lucas, Robert. "Econometric Policy Evaluation: A Critique." *The Philips Curve and Labour Markets*, edited by Karl Brunner and Alan Meltzer. *Carnegie-Rochester Conference Series on Public Policy*, vol 1, no. 1, 1976, pp. 19-46.

Mäki, Uskali. "Scientific realism as a challenge to economics (and vice versa)." *Journal of Economic Methodology*, vol. 18, no. 1, 2011, pp. 1-12.

McLeay, Michael, Amar Radia, and Ryland Thomas. "Money Creation in the Modern Economy." *Quarterly Bulletin*, vol. 14, Q1, 2014, pp. 14-27.

Menger, Carl. "On the Origin of Money." *The Economic Journal*, vol. 2, no. 6, 1892, pp. 239-55.

Minsky, Hyman. "Review: Frank Hahn's 'Money and Inflation'." *Journal of Post-Keynesian Economics*, vol. 6, no. 3, 1984, pp. 449-58.

Nakamoto, Satoshi. "Bitcoin: A Peer-to-Peer Electronic Cash System." *Bitcoin*, 2008,bitcoin.org/en/bitcoin-paper.

Olivecrona, Karl. *The Problem of the Monetary Unit*. Macmillan, 1957.

Omarova, Saule T. "New Tech v New Deal: Fintech as a Systemic Phenomenon." *Yale Journal on Regulation*, vol. 36, no. 2, 2019, pp. 735-93.

Pistor, Katharina. "A Legal Theory of Finance." *Journal of Comparative Economics*, vol. 41, no. 2, 2013, pp. 315-30.

Rogers, Colin. "The Conceptual Flaw in Microeconomic Foundations of Dynamic Stochastic General Equilibrium Models." *Review of Political Economy*, vol. 30, no. 4, 2018, pp. 72-83.

Schumpeter, Joseph. "Das Sozialprodukt und die Rechenpfennige." *Archiv für Sozialwissenschaft und Sozialpolitik*, vol. 44, 1917, pp. 627-715.

Searle, John. *Making the Social World*. Oxford University Press, 2010.

—. *The Construction of Social Reality*. Free Press, 1995.

Simmel, Georg. *The Philosophy of Money*. Translated by Tom Bottomore and David Frisby, Routledge, 1978.

Smit, J. P., Filip Buekins and Stan du Plessis. "Cigarettes, Dollars and Bitcoins - An Essay on the Ontology of Money." *Journal of Institutional Economics*, vol. 12, no. 2, 2016, pp. 327-47.

Smith, Barry. "Aristotle, Menger, Mises: An Essay in the Metaphysics of Economics." *History of Political Economic Annual Supplement*, vol. 22, 1990, pp. 263-88.

—, and John Searle. "The Construction of Social Reality: An Exchange." *John Searle's Ideas About Social Reality: Extensions, Criticisms, and Reconstructions,* edited by David Koepsell and Laurence Moss, Blackwell, 2003, pp. 285-310.

Weber, Beat. "What is 'Modern Money Theory' (MMT)?" *SUERF Policy Note*, no. 67, April 2019.

Wray, L. Randall. "Modern Money." *What is Money?*, by John Smithin, Routledge, 2000, pp. 42-66.

Beneath and Beyond the City:
The Multiple Faces of British Finance

Olivier Butzbach

INTRODUCTION

Among the most entrenched visions of modern capitalism stands the City, London's financial district. The City has come to epitomise first British financial imperialism, as British capital flooded the emerging economies of the late 19th century; and then, once the Empire was gone, the might of financial markets, both within and outside the United Kingdom. The City is, of course, a metonymy for the United Kingdom's financial services industry. The City of London refers to a territory of little more than a square mile within London (hence it being known, alternatively, as the "Square Mile") and is one of the 33 administrative districts constituting the metropolitan city (without initial capital letter) of London. But "The City" distinguishes itself from London's other 32 districts: it is not a borough but a county. In addition, the City of London is a corporation. Its governance is very peculiar and dates back centuries.

There is a lot to say about the spatial dimension of the City of London – what territory it includes beyond the administrative boundaries, the spatial relationships between the City and the broader metropolitan area, and the relationships between the City and other financial districts in the UK and elsewhere. However, this is not what this chapter is about.

The following pages, by contrast, deal with the metonymy itself – how it became taken for granted, what it says about how we view finance in general and the British financial system in particular, and, especially, what it does not say. To paraphrase Walter Bagehot, the famous editor of the *Economist* in the third quarter of the 19th century, the City is interesting for embodying finance as a "concrete reality"[1] – but a partly misleading embodiment, as is argued below.

The metonymy of the City encapsulates two very different characterisations of the British financial system. A first characterisation consists in the identification of the City with "financial markets"[2] – especially money markets – at the centre of Bagehot's book. Such characterisation is quite widely shared among financial economists, or scholars studying finance and financial systems in a comparative fashion. From this point of view, Britain is seen as epitomising "market-based" finance, by opposition to or contrast with "bank-based" finance usually associated with Germany and Japan (Allen and Gale; Demirgüç-Kunt and Levine). This classification matters as different qualities and/or levels of allocative efficiency are associated with each ideal-type (Levine; Beck and Levine). Such a view is obviously not completely wrong, especially when contrasting ideal-types. It is certainly true that, for instance, German capital markets have long been under-developed with respect to British ones; and that German universal banks had for a good part of the 20th century a tighter grip on the domestic economy than the large London clearing banks had on the British economy.

A second characterisation, which is less widespread among economists but more common, it seems, in cultural representations of the City,

---

1 In the opening sentences of "Lombard Street", Bagehot's seminal 1873 published collection of Economist articles, Bagehot wrote: "I venture to call this Essay 'Lombard Street,' and not the 'Money Market,' or any such phrase, because I wish to deal, and to show that I mean to deal, with concrete realities." (Bagehot 1)

2 A financial market can be defined as a decentralized system of resource allocation dealing with financial contracts and services.

treats the latter as the symbol of the concentration of financial power. This characterisation pervaded Victorian and Edwardian imagery, as Ranald Michie has shown (Michie, *Guilty Money*). English fiction reflected the mixed feelings held by the public regarding the City, which evolved over time. What did not change, however, was the association of the City with immense capital accumulation and increasingly larger (mostly joint-stock) organisations. Such imagery has persisted until recent times: in a 2014 study, Shaw showed how several post-2007 crisis British works of fiction contrasted the poverty and distress of several characters with greedy and powerful City institutions with a global reach. Such characterisation of London (and the City within it) as a global financial centre, populated with powerful financial institutions, is, again, not inaccurate: London is indeed one of the most important international financial centres in the world, together with New York. London, for instance, has the highest turnover in over-the-counter interest-rate derivative trading (one of the key derivatives markets). London also has the highest volume of foreign currency loans made each year by international banks; and is home to a handful of truly global banks (such as HSBC).

However, the double characterisation constituting the metonymy is no mere reflection, or generalisation of empirical experience – as Bagehot's argument seems to imply. It is a socially constructed image that is, in part, both contradictory and misleading. It is contradictory in that the first characterisation (the City as the embodiment of markets) clashes with the second image (the City as the symbol of concentrated power). It is misleading as the British financial system cannot be reduced to a system of markets, or to a tight network of all-powerful London-based financial institutions. Indeed, as the following pages will attempt to show, seeking a more accurate depiction of British finance forces us to look both beyond and beneath the City.

But why would we want to do that? Why, in other words, critically analyse the characterisation of the City summarised above? A simple answer is that such characterisations may be performative: as a cultural artefact, the City has necessarily had an impact on policy-makers' perspective. This simple argument builds on the more general view of economic (and especially financial) theories as performative (MacKenzie; see also Scherer and Marti). In the case of the City of London, the double characterisation described above was clearly an influential factor in two critical regulatory and political turning points in contemporary Britain: the Thatcherite "Big Bang" of 1986 and New Labour's "light touch" approach to financial regulation in the late 1990s and early 2000s (Daripa et al.). In both instances, there was (among policy-makers) great anxiety about the status of the City as a global financial centre; and the belief that unleashing financial markets' autonomous potential would constitute the basis for a successful growth strategy (Jessop; Sikka). The disastrous outcomes of such approaches, revealed by the 2007-08 financial crisis, thus show how necessary it is to rethink the place and role of the City in British finance.

THE 'CITY' IN BRITAIN:
A BRIEF HISTORICAL RETROSPECT

There is a broad consensus among economic historians on the pivotal role played by London-based financial institutions, and in particular financial institutions tied to the British capital markets, in the economic development of Great Britain over the past three centuries. Such a key role for a financial centre is a recurrent feature of modern capitalism, as many authors have shown (see, for instance, Arrighi). But the financial revolution in 17th-century Britain, centred around London, had a decisive impact on the country's subsequent fortunes. As a historian recently put it:

> Comprised of a long-term funded national debt, an active securities market, and a widely circulating credit currency, the modern financial system enabled England to create a powerful fiscal-military state, to forge a dominant

global empire, and to move in the direction of the Industrial Revolution faster than any other nation. (Wennerlind 1)

Furthermore, there is no doubt that the London capital markets were the central component of English, and then British, finance. In fact, the modern "financial revolution" in England is commonly attributed by historians to the joint development of a London-based market for corporate securities and a London-based market for government debt, both epitomised by the creation of the Bank of England in the late 17th century (see, in particular, Dickson). The stock market boom of the late 17th century accompanied the multiplication of joint-stock companies and the development of an active derivatives market in London. The city, which had been central to the country's trade industry, had a tight hold on the nascent financial industry. In fact, as Murphy has pointed out, "[m]ost participants in the financial market of the late seventeenth century lived either in or around London, and the majority of investors did travel to the City in order to complete their transactions" (Murphy 117). This situation certainly results from the high degree of political and economic centralisation characterising England at the time (Murphy; Porter).

The importance of London as a financial centre, established in the late 17th century, was constantly re-affirmed over the next three centuries – in particular, of course, during Britain's hegemony over the world economy between the late 18th century and the early 20th century (Arrighi). The period when Walter Bagehot directed and wrote in *The Economist* was probably the apex of the city's domination over world finance, which had started a century earlier, when London replaced Amsterdam as the centre of international financial networks of flows (Neal). London was briefly challenged by Paris as an international financial centre during the third quarter of the 19th century; but it re-established its pre-eminence soon after the 1871 end of the Franco-Prussian war, with its peculiar capacity to handle "an enormous body of transactions on a small monetary base" (Kindleberger 268). The definitive displacement of British hegemony over international financial markets, achieved by the United States by the end of World War II (see Arrighi), did not put an end to the City as an international financial centre. Indeed, London re-emerged as a global financial power with the rapid development of the Eurodollar bond market in the 1960s, and derivatives markets in subsequent decades (Michie, "A Financial Phoenix").

The renewed relevance of the city of London for domestic and global finance in the 21st century is also the fruit of a deep-seated transformation of modern capitalism that many scholars have dubbed "financialisation" (see, for instance, Epstein; and van der Zwan, for a recent review). Financialisation can be broadly defined as the growing importance of the financial sector and of financial transactions within the economy. Most financialisation scholars have interpreted it as the outcome of policy choices made in the 1970s by advanced economies to overcome the severe crisis these economies were undergoing (Krippner). As a result, the relative weight of financial profits out of total profits increased (Epstein), and non-financial companies increasingly targeted financial performance at the expense of the non-financial part of their business model. The British economy is certainly among the most financialised economies in the world. This situation can be illustrated with some data about the size and importance of the British financial industry: in 2017, the economic output of the British financial services industry has been estimated to amount to £119 billion, that is, 6.5% of total output – down from an all-time-high of 9.0% in 2009 (Rhodes); London accounted for about half of the financial industry's gross value added in 2017 – with the output of that industry accounting for 14% of London's total economic output, far above the national average (Rhodes).

Overall, there seems to be a strong continuity between the early constitution of the London-based capital markets in the late 17th century and the actual physiognomy of British finance today. However, there are key differences as well. One of these differences consists of the degree and nature of integration of London-based financial markets into global financial networks. A key to the success of the London financial markets in the age of Financial Revolution was their ability to tie domestic investment and speculation with domestic public debt and international trade finance – what Arrighi calls a "territorialist" state and a capitalist elite (Arrighi). By the late 20th century, by contrast, the City was much more geared towards world financial flows. By 2000, 40,000 workers were employed in London-based foreign banks (and foreign bank subsidiaries), against 25,000 who worked for domestic banks (Roberts). The international banking operations of UK-based banks dwarf their domestic banking operations; and the City of London has now become an important hub for offshore financial flows (Shaxson).

The City's greater tendency to look outward today does not reduce the salience of the double characterisation presented above, however. It is part and parcel of what Saskia Sassen has named "global cities" – major cities that have become simultaneously "highly concentrated command points for the world economy" and "key locations for finance" (Sassen 3). Yet this City-centred and market-based view of British finance is partial only, as the following sections aim to show.

BEYOND THE CITY: THE BRITISH STATE

"You might as well, or better, try to alter the English monarchy and substitute a republic, as to alter the present constitution of the English money market, founded on the Bank of England, and substitute for it a system in which each bank shall keep its own reserve", wrote Bagehot in the conclusion of his 1873 book (Bagehot 330). Throughout his studies of the British money market, indeed, Bagehot constantly pointed to the dependence of such markets on the Bank of England for their functioning. A broader view, within a longer time frame, confirms this impression. All financial historians cannot emphasise enough the central role played by "public" institutions such as the Bank of England (see, for a recent sample, Murphy; and Stasavage, *Public Debt*). But the Bank of England is, since 1997, formally independent from the British government. Before that date, the Bank depended on the British Treasury as much as money markets depended on the Bank of England – as, again, Bagehot put it: "[o]n the whole, therefore, the position of the Chancellor of the Exchequer in our Money Market is that of one who deposits largely in it, who created it, and who demoralised it" (111). There are, and were, tight links between the City and Westminster. These links have, of course, evolved over time, and the Bank of England did establish its autonomy from party politics in the course of its life. Autonomy from party politics did not imply, however, autonomy from the British state. In his history of banking and money in the UK, Collins did emphasise how much the Bank's prestige relied on its relationship with the state: the Bank "had been created out of the need for state finance, providing loans in return for the special privileges incorporated in its charter; and it continued to supply funds and handle the government's accounts" (Collins 169). The "privileges" Collins refers to include the monopoly of joint-stock banking in England and Wales conferred on the Bank of England in 1697 and further consolidated in 1707 (it was abolished in 1826); and the monopoly of legal tender attributed to Bank of England notes in 1833 (Collins).

Beyond the particular institution that was the Bank of England, which stood at the crossroads between the British state and the money markets (represented, at first, by the class of London merchants), London-based financial markets have historically been firmly embedded in what we may call a state-market nexus. First, the activities of the London stock exchange, in its first two centuries of activity, largely revolved around public (e.g. state) finance. As late as 1853, as Christiane Eisenberg notes, British government bonds still accounted for 70% of the trading volume on the stock exchange (70). Secondly, and more broadly, modern financial markets have pervasive institutional roots, starting with the legal organisational forms and financial contracts widely used in London. In other words, the "corporate capitalism" of the 20th century had Victorian origins, both in legal and cultural terms (Johnson). Perhaps more provocatively, in a study of British banking stability from 1800 to the current periods, John Turner argues that "politics [...] is the ultimate determinant of banking stability" (211).

Another critical take on the view of British financial capitalism as "market-based" is that, simply put, markets are antithetical to capitalism. This view was first neatly expressed by French historian Fernand

Braudel in his *Civilisation matérielle, économie et capitalisme* (1979 for the original French edition). Markets, in Braudel's view, are structured by horizontal communications, with a "degree of automatic coordination" that "usually links supply, demand and prices." By contrast, above this layer of the market economy "comes the zone of the anti-market, where the great predators roam and the law of the jungle operates" (Braudel 229). This zone, adds Braudel, is "the real home of capitalism." This view was drawn upon by intellectual successors to Braudel, such as Giovanni Arrighi, who further identified in financial centres the "fusion between state and capital" (Arrighi). This argument, then, brings us back to the first limitation of the "marketedness" of British finance exposed above.

As a matter of fact, it is the close interaction between capital accumulation processes and political power concentration processes that has characterised modern capitalism in the past three or four centuries. As Karl Polanyi put it, thus giving the metonymy discussed here particular salience, "[g]old standard and constitutionalism were the instruments which made *the voice of the City of London* heard in many smaller countries which had adopted these symbols of adherence to the new international order" (14; emphasis in the original). We should note, furthermore, that the emergence of modern nation-states, too, which can be considered as a process that is symmetrical to the emergence of capitalism, owes to a similar dialectical interaction between coercion and capital. Such is the thesis of Charles Tilly, who established a parallel between processes of concentration of capital, territorially associated with modern cities, on the one hand; and processes of concentration of coercion, territorially associated with modern states, on the other hand (Tilly). It is the combination of particular patterns of concentration of capital and coercive means that has given the modern nation-states their varying flavour. Interestingly, while in Tilly's framework high levels of capital concentration hinder subsequent nation-state building processes, London is precisely an exception in that "in England a substantial state formed relatively early despite the presence of a formidable trading city" (61).

A different, but complementary, argument was put forward more recently by David Stasavage, who has studied the interrelations between
the joint development of modern credit systems and representative assemblies in late medieval and early modern Europe (Stasavage, *Public
debt*; *States of Credit*). In Stasavage's account, the development of modern credit (and, by extension, financial) systems was predicated upon the
expansion of public (i.e. government) borrowing, which depended in
turn on the public's trust in the polity's capacity to monitor and discipline the borrower's behaviour. Hence the key importance of powerful
representative assemblies, precisely able to exert such power (Stasavage, *States of Credit*). Again, as in Tilly's case, such a framework does
not, at first sight, fit the British case – since Stasavage associated higher,
more efficient degrees of monitoring with the representative assemblies
typical of European medieval city states, which differed greatly from
territorial states such as France (Stasavage, *States of Credit*). Great Britain was, of course, a territorial state; but here again, the high powers
conferred upon a representative assembly early on were a British exception and enabled the "virtuous" joint development of public credit and
government borrowers' accountability at the level of the nation-state.
This view builds on the seminal article by North and Weingast on the
decisive benefits of the 1688 Glorious Revolution for the subsequent development of finance in 18th-century Britain (North and Weingast).

Late 20th-century financialisation did not fundamentally alter this dialectical relationship between markets and the state in British finance.
As mentioned above, several authors explained financialisation as the
outcome of government strategies set up to escape the stagflation of the
1970s. More specifically, successive Tory (and, after 1997, New Labour) governments encouraged the development of financial markets,
liberalized banking and brokerage, adopted pro-business regulatory reforms (Sikka; Jessop), and directly participated in the financialisation of
public goods, such as land (Christophers).

Thus, finance in the UK is not (only) market-based, circumscribing
the first characterisation implied in the City metonymy, as argued in the
introduction. However, the arguments presented above do not help to

dispel the notion of a City-centred financial industry. To do so, one needs to turn one's attention to the actual diversity, organisational and territorial, beneath the City of London.

BENEATH THE CITY: THE DIVERSITY OF BRITISH FINANCE

Two features of British finance further circumscribe the descriptive accuracy of the "City of London" metonymy as far as the second characterisation is concerned. First, the City has not always been as hegemonic over British finance as it may appear today. It is true that British financial services today cluster around regional centres, with London proving the most attractive regional cluster in the 1990s (Pandit et al.), and that the geographical concentration of financial services in London has not abated in the wake of the 2007-08 crisis (Wójcik and MacDonald-Korth)[3]. Nevertheless, the history of British finance in the past three centuries is also the story of successful regional financial centres and local banks. As Collins argues, "until well into the second half of the nineteenth century the distinctive feature of the typical English provincial bank [...] was that its business was overwhelmingly local in nature" (22).

A second limitation arises out of the persistent organisational diversity of British finance. In other words, the British financial industry is constituted by a multitude of organisational forms, each of which carry or embody distinct institutional logics. Organisational forms, in the organisational theory literature, are usually construed as sets of features (the particular governance structure of an organisation, its legal status and mandate, its core business model) that attribute a particular identity to an organisation and hence make it belong to a specific population of organisations. In the British context, now dominated by large joint-stock

---

3   In particular, these authors find that London's share of financial employment has increased between 2008 and 2012, from 32% to 34%.

companies, the financial industry was heterogeneous for long periods of time, accommodating the presence, at the side of joint-stock banks, stock brokers and insurance companies, of mutual financial institutions such as building societies and mutual insurers, as well as Trustees savings banks (Casu and Gall).

Building societies are an especially interesting type of financial institution, given that they represent the polar opposite to the large London-based clearing banks commonly associated with the British financial system. Building societies, which first appeared in Birmingham in the 1770s, were mutual mortgage lenders; they underwent a very steady rise in numbers during the 19th century, and a rapid increase in members during the 20th century – especially after the 1930s (Bellman).

By the early 1970s British building societies had reached a dominant position in mortgage lending, holding very high market shares throughout the decade, reaching a peak of 82% in 1978. However, the strong position of building societies on various key segments of retail financial markets underwent significant decline in the late 1980s and, most importantly, during the 1990s. On the mortgage lending market new forays by banks, unburdened by the restrictive regulation imposed by monetary authorities in the previous decades, slowly eroded societies' market shares. This erosion accelerated in the late 1980s and late 1990s, due to the transfer of the mortgage assets of de-mutualized societies after a 1986 reform encouraged them to do so.

Today (as of early 2019), building societies have not completely disappeared; there are 42 of them (against hundreds in the 1970s); they are mostly small in size, with the exception of Nationwide, the largest mutual lender in the UK. Their mortgage market share is small by comparison with its level in the 1970s and 1980s, but it is still very significant, with a 25.6% share of gross mortgage lending in 2018.[4] Building societies thus epitomise persistent diversity within the British financial system. Although such diversity has clearly receded since the 1970s, thus becoming an issue for policy-makers in the wake of the 2007-08 crisis,

---

4   Source: Building Societies Association.

it has resisted the pressures of homologation and competitive isomorphism. Such diversity continues to undermine a City-centred view of British finance.

CONCLUSION

The City is a powerful metonymy – a metaphor for the power of finance in modern capitalism. It also encapsulates a double characterisation of the British financial system, simultaneously seen as, on the one hand, the supreme embodiment of the power of markets and, on the other, the symbol of the concentration of capital in the hands of a few global institutions. This twin characterisation is potentially contradictory as well as misleading, as has been shown here.

In particular, British finance is not completely market-based nor is it exclusively centred around London-based joint-stock behemoths. British finance expresses the strong interrelations of state and market and exhibits persistent diversity despite isomorphic pressures. This, I argue here, calls for a more careful characterisation of British finance and points to the importance of historicising both the material side of imagined economies as well as their symbolic aspects.

REFERENCES

Allen, Franklin, and Douglas Gale. *Comparing Financial Systems*. The MIT Press, 2001.

Arrighi, Giovanni. *The Long Twentieth Century: Money, Power, and the Origins of Our Times*. Verso, 1994.

Bagehot, Walter. *Lombard Street. A Description of the Money Market.* 1873. John Wiley & Sons, 1999.

Beck, Thorsten, and Ross Levine. "Industry Growth and Capital Allocation: Does Having a Market- or Bank-Based System Matter?" *Journal of Financial Economics*, vol. 64, no. 2, 2002, pp. 147-80.

Bellman, Sir Harold. *The Thrifty Three Millions. A Study of the Building Society Movement and the Story of the Abbey Road Society*. The Abbey Road Building Society, 1935.

Braudel, Fernand. *Civilization and Capitalism, 15th-18th Century. Vol. III: The Perspective of the World*. Harper and Row, 1982.

Casu, Barbara, and Andrew Gall. *Building Societies in the Financial Services Industry*. Springer, 2017.

Christophers, Brett. "The State and Financialization of Public Land in the United Kingdom." *Antipode,* vol. 49, no.1, 2017, pp. 62-85.

Collins, Michael. *Money and Banking in the UK. A History.* Routledge, 1988.

Daripa, Arup, Sandeep Kapur, and Stephen Wright. "Labour's Record on Financial Regulation." *Oxford Review of Economic Policy*, vol. 29, no. 1, 2013, pp. 71-94.

Demirgüç-Kunt, Asli, and Ross Levine. *Bank-Based and Market-Based Financial Systems: Cross-Country Comparisons*. The World Bank, 1999.

Dickson, Peter G. M. *The Financial Revolution in England: a Study in the Development of Public Credit, 1688-1756*. Routledge, 1993.

Eisenberg, Christiane. *The Rise of Market Society in England, 1066-1800*. Berghahn Books, 2013.

Epstein, Gerald A., editor. *Financialization and the World Economy*. Edward Elgar Publishing, 2005.

Jessop, Bob. "Neoliberalism, Finance-Dominated Accumulation and Enduring Austerity: A Cultural Political Economy Perspective." *Social Policy in Times of Austerity: Global Economic Crisis and the New Politics of Welfare*, edited by Kevin Farnsworth and Zoë Irving, Policy Press, 2015, pp. 87-112.

Johnson, Paul. *Making the Market: Victorian Origins of Corporate Capitalism*. Cambridge University Press, 2010.

Kindleberger, Charles P. *A Financial History of Western Europe*. Routledge, 1984.

Krippner, Greta R. *Capitalizing on Crisis. The Political Origins of the Rise of Finance*. Harvard University Press, 2011.

Levine, Ross. "Bank-Based or Market-Based Financial Systems: Which is Better?" *Journal of Financial Intermediation*, vol. 11, no. 4, 2002, pp. 398-428.

MacKenzie, Donald. *An Engine, not a Camera: How Financial Models Shape Markets*. MIT Press, 2008.

Michie, Ranald C. *Guilty Money: The City of London in Victorian and Edwardian Culture, 1815-1914*. Routledge, 2015.

—. "A Financial Phoenix: the City of London in the Twentieth Century." *London and Paris as International Financial Centres in the Twentieth Century*, edited by Eric Bussière and Youssef Cassis. Oxford University Press, 2005, pp. 15-41.

Murphy, Anne. *The Origins of the English Financial Markets: Investment and Speculation Before the South Sea Bubble*. Cambridge University Press, 2009.

Neal, Larry. *The Rise of Financial Capitalism: International Capital Markets in the Age of Reason*. Cambridge University Press, 1993.

North, Douglass C., and Barry R. Weingast. "Constitutions and Commitment: The Evolution of Institutions Governing Public Choice in Seventeenth-Century England." *The Journal of Economic History*, vol. 49, no. 4, 1989, pp. 803-32.

Pandit, Naresh R., Gary A. S. Cook, and G. M. Peter Swann. "The Dynamics of Industrial Clustering in British Financial Services." *Service Industries Journal*, vol. 21, no. 4, 2001, pp. 33-61.

Polanyi, Karl. *The Great Transformation*. Beacon Press, 1957.

Porter, Roy. *London: A Social History*. Harvard University Press, 1998.

Rhodes, Chris. *Financial Services: Contribution to the UK Economy*. House of Commons Library Briefing Paper SN06193, 2018.

Roberts, Richard. "London as an International Financial Centre, 1980-2000: Global Powerhouse or Wimbledon EC2?" *London and Paris as International Financial Centres in the Twentieth Century*, edited by Eric Bussière and Youssef Cassis. Oxford University Press, 2005, pp. 287-312.

Sassen, Saskia. *The Global City. New York, London, Kyoto*. Princeton University Press, 1991.

Scherer, Andreas G., and Emilio Marti. "The Normative Foundation of Finance: How Misunderstanding the Role of Financial Theories Distorts the Way We Think about the Responsibility of Financial Economists." *Learning from the Global Financial Crisis: Creatively, Reliably, and Sustainably*, edited by Paul Shrivastava and Matt Statler, Stanford University Press, 2012, pp. 260-90.

Shaw, Katy. "'Capital' City: London, Contemporary British Fiction and the Credit Crunch." *The Literary London Journal*, vol. 11, no. 1, 2014, pp. 44-53.

Shaxson, Nicholas. *Treasure Islands: Uncovering the Damage of Offshore Banking and Tax Havens*. St. Martin's Press, 2011.

Sikka, Prem. "The Corrosive Effects of Neoliberalism on the UK Financial Crises and Auditing Practices: A Dead-End for Reforms." *Accounting Forum*, Elsevier, vol. 39, no. 1, 2015, pp. 1-18.

Stasavage, David. *States of Credit: Size, Power, and the Development of European Polities*. Princeton University Press, 2011.

—. *Public Debt and the Birth of the Democratic State: France and Great Britain 1688-1789*. Cambridge University Press, 2003.

Tilly, Charles. *Coercion, Capital, and European States, AD 990-1992*. Basil Blackwell, 1990.

Turner, John D. *Banking in Crisis: The Rise and Fall of British Banking Stability, 1800 to the Present*. Cambridge University Press, 2014.

Van der Zwan, Natascha. "Making Sense of Financialization." *Socio-Economic Review*, vol. 12, no. 1, 2014, pp. 99-129.

Wennerlind, Carl. *Casualties of Credit. The English Financial Revolution, 1620-1720.* Harvard University Press, 2011.

Wójcik, Dariusz, and Duncan MacDonald-Korth. "The British and the German Financial Sectors in the Wake of the Crisis: Size, Structure and Spatial Concentration." *Journal of Economic Geography*, vol. 15, no. 5, 2015, pp. 1033-54.

A Nation of Shopkeepers? The Idealised High Street in Brexit Britain

Rebecca Bramall

In the decade since the global financial crisis of 2007-8, thousands of shops have closed in high streets across the United Kingdom. Wage stagnation, rising business rates and competition from online retailers have been blamed for the consequent "death of the high street" (Marsh). Media coverage of this demise – illustrated by pictures of empty, fly-posted retail units – has tracked the transformation of formerly vibrant locations into desolate spaces recolonised by the 'wrong' sort of retail activity – charity shops, betting shops and pawnbrokers. These representations convey a strong sense of the retail industry and as well as the UK economy at large undergoing a period of change, "laid bare for us all to see" (Morrison).

Since June 2016, when the UK voted to leave the European Union, the fate of Britain's troubled high streets has become freighted with deeper significance. The UK's relationship with the EU – an 'anchor' of Britain's economic model for over four decades (Weldon 12) – became an object of interrogation and uncertainty, placing Britain's economic future in question. Brexit was a singular event that appeared "to both disrupt and open up possibilities", but it can also be understood as a more diffuse phenomenon that "surfaces across multiple ordinary scenes and situations", instituting a period of intense and highly contested future-making (Anderson and Wilson 291-2).

This chapter investigates the opportunities to imagine Britain's economic future that have proliferated in this moment of Brexit. It does so through the site of the high street and its *idealisation*. The dominant narrative of the high street's decline competes for our attention with a very different set of representations that portray renewed and thriving examples of these places (Griffiths). These 'model' high streets have been seized upon as evidence that it is possible to revive town centre shopping districts and the communities that are sustained by them. Through an analysis of various material and textual instances of the idealised high street, I investigate this site as a point of entry into contemporary economic imaginaries. What kinds of desires, hopes and expectations can be traced in the idealised high street? And what do these aspirations tell us about broader economic imaginaries in Brexit Britain?

This chapter introduces and contextualises three instances of the idealised high street and identifies their shared tropes. I go on to argue that the site of the idealised high street supports two related but ultimately conflicting economic imaginaries that afford progressive and reactionary visions of economic organisation and solidarity in alternative post-Brexit futures. In the final part of the chapter I draw on my analysis of the idealised high street to foreground some of the obstacles that exist to the radical democratisation of local economies.

IMAGINING THE ECONOMY

As others have noted, a concern with the 'imagined economy', or 'economic imaginaries', should not be dismissed as immaterial or trivial (Clarke 17). It follows from a recognition that economic activities cannot be "conducted independently of systems of meaning and norms" (Ray and Sayer 6), and from an intention to create a space for the interrogation of those signifying practices. 'Imaginaries' have been defined as "semiotic systems that frame individual subjects' lived experience", and so an 'economic imaginary' is a system that "gives meaning and shape to the 'economic' field" (Jessop 344). John Clarke observes that the 'invention' of the economic "creates the conditions for things called economies to be imagined in different ways, involving different architectures, elements, dynamics, figures and embodiments" (19). This chapter is particularly concerned with the alternative possibilities prefigured in 'emergent imaginaries' (Birch), and in disentangling the co-existence of related economic imaginaries (Swartz).

There are countless practices, discourses, representations and spaces which might be studied in order to gain a deeper picture of economic imaginaries in Brexit Britain. This chapter focuses on a particularly rich site of meaning: the *idealised high street*. In a context in which the complexity of financial markets is understood to contribute to global economic instability, and in which economic globalisation is widely cited as a driver of fiscal challenges, the significance of the local, human scale of the high street is palpable. High streets are spaces in which citizens habitually engage in tangible economic transactions. These transactions are cognitively graspable in a way that national and global scales of economic activity are often not, and so they provide an essential point of entry into public debate about 'the economy'. Indeed, high streets are often portrayed as representing the economy in microcosm. A tendency towards the fetishisation of high streets in reporting on business and economics presents a misleading picture of their representativeness of the broader economy and of the contribution of retail to GDP, yet it points to the significance of high streets in contemporary economic imaginaries.

As Sam Griffiths notes, high streets are significant both for *what they do* – for their material, functional attributes – and *what they mean* – their symbolic resonances (32). Shopping streets, and the commercial activities that they epitomise, have long played a role in British national identity and ideas about economic well-being (Benson and Ugolini). In more recent years the high street has emerged as an object of "collective concern" (McDonald and Cassidy 307) bound up with public debate about the fostering of 'community' in towns and cities (Hubbard; Watson and

Wells). Shoppers, retailers and policymakers alike perceive the high street as 'the glue that binds a community together' (Fletcher et al. 485). In their efforts to formulate solutions to its decline, politicians, urban planners and commentators (Alakeson; Harris; Sikka) recognise and respond to the '*generative* qualities' (Griffiths 41) of the high street, underscoring the centrality of this cultural and economic site in contemporary economic imaginaries and its status as a model of the national economy in miniature. The high street, then, is more than just a geographical location in which retail activity takes place. It can instead be understood as a site that opens up opportunities to envision and enact social, political, and economic change.

NOSTALGIA FOR THE HIGH STREET

The current wave of intense focus on high streets and their perceived decline is often accompanied with expressions of nostalgia for these locations as they are imagined to have functioned in the past – whether in the 'golden age' before the financial crisis (McDonald and Cassidy), in post-war society (Hubbard), or further back in time (Watson and Wells). This nostalgia is manifested, for instance, in the way that new and existing types of commercial activity cultivate a nostalgic retail aesthetic (Bramall), or incorporate references to the past into their rationale for conducting business (Hubbard). It has also been traced in research informants' discussion about how shopping districts have changed (Watson and Wells) and their aspirations for the future of these locations (Fletcher et al.).

Nostalgia for the high street of the past is not a new phenomenon. It can be located in a longer history of collective expressions of yearning for the way we imagine ourselves to have shopped in bygone times (Benson and Ugolini). As the cultural historian Raphael Samuel explains, shops have been cultivating a 'heritage' feel for decades (Samuel). The notion of the 'period' shopping street developed in the museum sector in the 1930s and by the 1960s had become a leading attraction at museums and theme parks. In the late 1970s the renovation of Covent Garden in central London introduced features such as Victorian street lamps and cobbled paving to the market. Samuel argues that in these decades, a "new version of the national past" began to offer "more points of access to 'ordinary people'", and that shopping accordingly enjoyed "a new visibility" (159-60).

Samuel interprets 'period' shopping in the 1970s and 80s as a form of "living history", and as interrelated with the preoccupation of the baby boomer generation with "lifestyles" (196). Yet he is keen to challenge a contemporary critique of 'heritage' advanced by historians such as Patrick Wright and Robert Hewison, who disparage such modes of historical engagement as delivering a sanitised, inauthentic and invariably reactionary picture of the past (Wright; Hewison; Samuel 259-71). Samuel is both considerate of the tendency for 'heritage' to be appropriated by conservatism and sensitive to the opportunities for "historical reflection and thought" (271) that these popular, engaging, and often embodied modes of encounter promote. He is ultimately confident of the openness of the past to political resignification: "there are no historical propositions", he argues, "which are insulated from contrary readings" (164).

Griffiths offers a different perspective on the imbrication of the past and present in the space of the high street, or the question of "how the past of a town, city or suburb relates to its future" (33). He draws attention to a tendency in debate about the value of 'heritage' – or the historical residues contained in high streets – to insist on the discrepancy between past and present. This view is challenged through an investigation of the function of the historical built environment (considered in the long term, rather than more recent historical eras) in sustaining "communal continuity" through "spatial co-presence" (40). Griffiths concludes that the high street "is not a repository of static meanings to be toyed with but rather a source of time-space orientations towards the world that afford social memory" (50).

This chapter draws on these perspectives in my own analysis of the activation of the historical past in the idealised high street, and its function in the 'making present of diverse futures' in Brexit Britain.

THE IDEALISED HIGH STREET: THREE INSTANCES

Samuel's mode of analysis frequently moves between the discussion of different kinds of illustrations and examples, from photographs to street furniture. In a similar way, I want to introduce and focus upon three specific instances of the idealised high street, which – along with further contextualisation – will serve to foreground certain common tropes.

The High Street is a children's picture book written and illustrated by Edinburgh-based artist Alice Melvin. The story's protagonist, a girl called Sally, sets out on a shopping trip in search of a list of somewhat obscure items – a yellow rose, a garden hose, a cockatoo, a tin kazoo, and so on. Arriving at 'The High Street', she visits a series of traditional shops, including a toy shop, a greengrocer, a hardware shop, and a florist. Each double page spread features text on the left – composed in verse – and an illustration of a shop front on the right, which can be opened to reveal an interior depicting Sally's retail encounter. Sally succeeds in acquiring most of the items on her list, but is disappointed when she is unable to buy a yellow rose in the florist. At the end of the story she leaves the high street with 'memories' of yellow roses flowering in the adjacent public park. Period high streets are popular settings in children's picture books (Griffiths), and Melvin's illustrations evoke classic texts by authors such as Janet and Allan Ahlberg.

Bishopthorpe Road (or 'Bishy Road') is a shopping street in York, in the north of England. York is a walled city with two universities and a population of about 205,000. Bishopthorpe Road is located to the southwest of the city, outside the city centre, and the area has been a shopping district for at least 150 years (Clements Hall). It was named winner of the 'Great British High Street of the Year' in 2015, in a scheme run by the Department for Communities and Local Government. It has been the focus of significant and sustained media attention, with one headline declaring it a model of "how to bring a high street back from the dead" (Rushby, "How to Bring a High Street"). Bishopthorpe Road is both a real place – with material, functional attributes – and also an *imagined* place that has been held up as an ideal in extensive media representation of its high street.

The third instance of the idealised high street is contained in a planning document on shop front design issued in 2016 by the 'Regeneration and Growth' section of the London Borough of Waltham Forest, an area of northeast London. Aimed at encouraging more people to visit the borough's high streets, the document gives advice on "how to achieve a high quality, attractive shop front". It is illustrated by examples of 'good practice' from shopping districts in the borough, including Leyton High Street, Walthamstow Village, and Higham Hill Road. Many borough councils across the UK make similar guidance available to businesses in their area.

What common elements do these instances share? And what do they tell us about the idealised high street? First of all, these are all examples, in different ways, of idealised high streets as 'period' streets. In each case there is repeated referencing and valorisation of the past, although no particular period is preferred or consistently evoked. The shops in Melvin's book adopt different architectural styles dating from the mid-19th century through to the 1930s. Edwardian and Victorian shop fronts dominate, with some Art Deco motifs. Each illustration incorporates period features such as pilasters, corbels, mullions, fluting, plaques, and clocks. Stories celebrating Bishopthorpe Road emphasise its history of trading, dating back to the 1870s. Waltham Forest's planning guidelines attach great importance to the historical built environment through an emphasis on the value of "original features" and "traditional elements".

These are not exactly the 'period' streets that Samuel describes: they are not actively seeking to recreate and immerse the visitor in a particular era from the past. Instead, there is an alignment with Griffiths's observation that British high streets tend to "escape definition in terms of conventional historical periods" (35). These instances of the idealised high street share an aspiration to remove certain markers of the present-day from shop fronts, so that, in so far as it is possible, all that is left is 'period'. In this sense, Melvin's high street is a perfect illustration of Waltham Forest's planning guidelines, and many of the shops in Bishopthorpe Road have been renewed in ways that would also meet with the council's approval. The aspiration to remove markers of the present-day also extends into the street itself, where pedestrian, car-free space is favoured. Ice cream is sold opposite Melvin's toy shop from a vending tricycle, while in the Waltham Forest planning guidelines, an apron-wearing, retro bicycle-riding delivery boy makes an appearance outside a strongly endorsed delicatessen.

Second, these instances of the high street present shopkeeping as a decent and even aspirational way of earning a living. Retailers have historically been conferred an ambiguous and often maligned social status, with "trade and shopkeeping [...] generally associated with notions of greed, pettiness and narrow-mindedness" in the 19th and 20th centuries (Benson and Ugolini 6). Samuel contends that in the "living history" of late 20th-century heritage culture, labour and industry began to be "retrospectively dignified". The shopkeeper was "rehabilitated and given an honoured place" in the national story, becoming "an emblem of 'knowledgeable and friendly service'" (161). The shopkeepers of Bishopthorpe Road embody this rehabilitated image. In press coverage of the street's fortunes, they are portrayed as enterprising, determined and civic-minded, "used to rolling up their sleeves and getting on with it" (Rushby, "It Could be Terrible"). Fascia signs feature first and second names: titles such as Millie's Fruit & Veg, McBride's Opticians, and Thomas the Baker communicate the status of these shops as small, family enterprises, with owners who are proud to put their name to their business. In Melvin's high street a commitment to the locality and community is emphasised through the depiction of shopkeepers' quarters above their stores. The broader context is one in which Adam Smith's description of the English as a 'nation of shopkeepers' has been recuperated by Conservative politicians such as Iain Duncan Smith, who has praised shopkeepers for modelling 'entrepreneurial spirit' (Dominiczak).

Third, these instances of the high street express a strong commitment to independence, individuality, and uniqueness, qualities set in contrast with the blandness and homogeneity that are associated with big brands and retail chains. These types of businesses are of course entirely absent from Melvin's book, while they are tolerated in the Waltham Forest planning guidelines only so long as they do not overly 'dominate', or break with the 'cohesiveness' of the street. The Bishopthorpe Road traders proudly proclaim that their shops are 90% independent. This feeling that 'independent' is best, and that big brands and chain stores are an unwanted presence on the idealised high street, can also be readily evidenced elsewhere. For example, in 2017 the book retailer Waterstones opened a series of unbranded bookshops – named 'Southwold Books', 'The Blackheath Bookshop' and so on – in high streets across the UK. Managing Director of the chain James Daunt justified their approach by explaining that these stores were opening in "quite sensitive high streets with predominantly independent retailers on them [...]. If you want to enhance a high-street you need to act as an independent" (Sayid).

Fourth, these instances conceive of the ideal high street as delivering something more than retail opportunities. Media representations of Bishopthorpe Road ascribe its revival to the fostering of community spirit. Central to the narrative of the street's recuperation is the closure of the road to traffic for a community street party (Rushby, "How to Bring a High Street"). Likewise, Melvin incorporates community spaces into her vision of the high street, with activities such as band practice and puppet shows in evidence. An emphasis on 'social places' can also be found in the 2011 Portas review – a report on Britain's high streets carried out by a celebrity businesswoman. Portas describes her vision for high streets as "destinations for socialising, culture, health and wellbeing, creativity and learning" (14), practices that we see depicted and given space in the idealised high street.

ECONOMIC IMAGINARIES IN BREXIT BRITAIN

Ben Anderson and Helen Wilson note that the moment of Brexit, inaugurated by the outcome of the referendum in 2016, is one in which 'diverse futures' have been made present, often in ways that involve the activation of the past. These futures "open up an opportunity to reflect on how spaces for new and emerging forms of solidarity, both progressive and otherwise, are created, reworked, or closed down" (Anderson and Wilson 293). The idealised high street can be understood as an example of such a space, and specific instances of the tendencies I have described have been interpreted as fostering reactionary forms of solidarity. In a scathing response to Waltham Forest's shop front scheme, Owen Hatherley has criticised the borough's insistence on a unifying retro aesthetic, which has the effect – he claims – of purging the urban high street of its diversity, conviviality and appeal. "London streets don't need to look like a historically illiterate retcon of a 1940s that never happened", he argues, "they're fine looking like what they are, hugely successful experiments in multiculturalism" (Hatherley).

While Hatherley offers a valid insight, it is worth testing the limits of this argument. Does the space of the idealised high street *only* serve to engender reactionary forms of solidarity? And are 'period' settings such as those that characterise the idealised high street *inherently* generative of such outcomes? In what follows, I pay close attention to the centrality of the idealised high street in contemporary economic imaginaries, emphasising the extent to which diverse constituencies make imaginative investments in this site. I argue that it can be understood to support conflicting imaginaries that afford both reactionary *and* progressive visions of economic organisation and solidarity in alternative post-Brexit futures. Yet, as I will discuss at the end of this chapter, a certain identity and overlap between these alternative visions helps us to recognise the exclusions that are perpetuated in both economic imaginaries.

A Nice Row of Shops: The High Street in Little England

It is not difficult to discern elements of the idealised high street that support visions of the future that are exclusionary, protectionist, reactionary, and indeed racist. We might begin by foregrounding certain normative statements about the social that are asserted through the idealisation of the high street. The types of shops, the products that they sell, the people that sell them, and the people that buy them, all describe a world and imply particular shared values. Bishopthorpe Road is described in one news story as 'an almost perfect parade'. That perfection is achieved when the right selection of unique, independent stores – each representing a distinct, 'traditional' trade – are assembled in a cohesive way: the butcher, baker, greengrocer, toy shop and so on. The assemblage of these traders serves to project a wider community of high street users who share an opinion of what the 'perfect parade' should offer, because they share values and ways of living. They need the same kinds of products and use them in the same kinds of ways. It is "a nice row of shops run by nice people for nice people" (Haywood).

'Nice', here, is a way of talking about cultural and economic capital: the shared values and ways of living endorsed by the street are tied up with affluence and middle-class taste. Elsewhere, however, idealised high streets erect exclusionary borders that operate along both classed and racialised lines. Waltham Forest's shop front design document elaborates key design considerations by reference to a drawing of a 'traditional shop front' and a series of visual examples, each designated an example of 'good' or 'bad' practice. The shops identified as examples of poor practice are invariably those serving a particular ethnic community. They are deemed to lack the requisite 'respect' for original architectural features, and are criticised because they appear 'cluttered', 'seek undue attention', and 'dominate their surroundings unnecessarily'. In this way, the design considerations expressed in this document communicate hierarchies of value, quality, and belonging that are bound up with broader nationalist imaginaries.

It would be highly misleading to suggest that any of these three instances of the idealised high street anticipate an explicitly racist vision for the future. On the contrary, Melvin's book offers an attentively multicultural depiction of the high street, incorporating shops run by people of apparently different ethnicities and visited by a diversity of customers. It is important to recognise, however, that such acts of inclusion are circumscribed by the terms and terrain on which they are made, which include the foregrounding and valorisation of the 'period' qualities of the built environment. Writing about 'micropubs' – very small public houses, which have been celebrated in visions of high street regeneration – Hubbard construes their "socially and culturally exclusive" dimension (20) as fostered in part through the design and decoration of these spaces, which are "characterised by artefacts and signs which invoke banal nationalism" (17). Offers of inclusion in the high street are also framed by the resurgence of a narrative of British self-sufficiency and calls for "ethnocentric consumption" (Lekakis). While this is a highly contested terrain of discourse – struggled over by nationalists, free marketeers, and environmentalists – it is often informed by a highly selective recollection of Britain's interrelationship with, and dependence upon, other countries and places, and in particular with the countries that made up its former Empire (Virdee and McGeever).

'Our Town': The High Street in a Democratised Economy

In addition to the reactionary vision of economic solidarity I have just detailed, the idealised high street also supports an alternative and much more progressive imaginary, and serves as a site of investment in hopes and desires for a radically reconfigured economy. These desires can be traced, for a start, in the positive vision of good, meaningful labour that the idealised high street nurtures. As I have already discussed, the idealised high street configures shopkeeping as a decent and civic-minded way of earning a living. This model of autonomy over one's working life offers a sharp point of contrast with other present-day media narratives about employment conditions in the United Kingdom, with their

tales of exhausted warehouse workers and destitute food delivery drivers. An emphasis on autonomy, control, and meaningful influence over
the economy can also be traced in the assertion (in all three instances) of
the more-than-economic value of retail activity to a local community,
and – in the case of Bishopthorpe Road – is extended to explicit engagement with the social ownership movement (Clements Hall). Finally, the
status of the idealised high street as an imagined microcosm of a broader
national economy means that it is a site through which the challenge of
combating wealth extraction by multinationals can be defined and addressed at a local level. London Borough of Waltham Forest, for instance, express a commitment to "retaining more wealth in the borough"
(13) in their planning guidance document.

   These tentative investments in models and practices that might transform local economies and communities resonate very strongly with the
Labour Party's current 'institutional turn', which has been defined in
terms of an "emerging new political economy [that] is circulatory and
place-based" (Guinan and O'Neill, "From Community Wealth"). For
Joe Guinan and Martin O'Neill, "decentralised public control of the
economy" could offer a means of co-opting Brexiteers' aspiration to
'take back control': it could "reconstitute the basis for democratic participation by giving people real decision-making power over the forces
that affect their lives" (Guinan and O'Neill, "The Institutional Turn" 10).
A widely discussed example of this new political economy is the so-
called Preston model (Guinan and O'Neill, "From Community
Wealth"), named after the town in the Northwest where the council have
introduced local wealth-building strategies. 'Anchor' institutions such
as colleges, housing associations and universities have been encouraged
to contract local companies, generating a multiplier effect: "pounds circulate and recirculate throughout the local economy, creating jobs which
in turn lead to more spending on goods and services, which then leads
to the creation of more jobs, and so on" (Hanna et al.). The council has
also supported co-operatives and other alternative forms of ownership
that deliver opportunities for workers to "participate in the economic decisions that affect their lives and the future of their city" (Hanna et al.).

The Preston model itself has been recognised as an "important form of prefiguration", and has been construed as a template which can help people to "imagine, experience, and get involved with systemic economic transformation" (Guinan and O'Neill, "From Community Wealth" 390). Because of its centrality to everyday economic imaginaries and its status as an imagined microcosm of a broader local or national economy, the site of the high street could also provide a terrain for the elaboration of radical ideas such as social ownership or community wealth building.

BEYOND THE HIGH STREET

Guinan and O'Neill describe community wealth building as "a left alternative to both extractive neoliberalism and xenophobic nationalism" ("From Community Wealth" 383). Should we be surprised, then, that the idealised high street provides the imaginative resources to expound both their radical vision and a reactionary economic nationalism? James Meek has argued that it is a mistake to assume that "'good' localism (the ideal of the 'thriving local community', locally sourced food, preservation of vernacular local architecture and the traditional local landscape) can be neatly separated from 'bad' localism (hostility to immigrants and new ways of doing things)" (16). Similarly, reactionary and progressive economic imaginaries can be fostered on the shared terrain of the idealised high street. The challenge, then, is to identify the obstacles that exist to the left's annexation of the site of the high street – and discourses of localism more generally – for the purpose of elaborating a radical economic vision. The analysis of idealisations of the high street initiated in this chapter can help us to recognise some of the barriers that exist to the radical democratisation of local economies.

One of the most pressing issues is the question of *whose* ideal is represented in *The High Street*, Bishopthorpe Road, and Waltham Forest's planning guidance, and in a more generalised idealisation of the high street. Who gets to desire and imaginatively invest in the high street and local economies at large? Who gets to debate "the kind of high street they would like" (Griffiths 39)? It is clear from my analysis that the idealised high street is a site in which affluent constituencies' desires are prioritised and in which classed and racialised exclusions are perpetuated. The identity and overlap between the alternative visions I have sketched out – the 'bad' localism of the Little Englander imaginary, and the 'good' localism of the Preston model – help us to recognise the exclusions in operation when it comes to the preferred subjects of dominant economic imaginaries. As Guinan and O'Neill note, social and economic inequalities prevent certain citizens from participation in the collective imagination of shared futures: "economic instability precludes active determination of a community's economic development, making the ambition to shape our collective future seem unattainable" ("From Community Wealth" 389). Those who seek the radical democratisation of the economy must therefore instigate democratic participation in *acts of imagination* vis-à-vis the economy. They must identify new ways of articulating and representing socially and economically marginalised subjects' desires for their local high streets and communities (Watson and Wells), and of bringing these imaginaries into dialogue with dominant idealisations.

My analysis also points to the limitations of the model of the high street as a microcosm of the local or national economy. Suzanne Hall has noted the tendency for 'the local' to be treated as a "confined territorial entity where parochial concerns are legitimised over broader concerns" (2585). Relatedly, the high street is fetishised in contemporary economic imaginaries to the extent that the significance of retail is overemphasised, and the economic transactions that shopping involves can appear disconnected from the wider economy. In order to support proposals for the radical democratisation of local economies, it will be necessary to develop a vision of the idealised high street that decentres the spaces and practices of retail while bringing a more extensive range of economic processes into focus. Emergent research on the institutional turn emphasises the importance of institutions that are publicly owned or working for the collective good. While the site of the high street and the transactions that take place in it provide a tangible point of entry into public debate about 'the economy', it is imperative to build a vision of local economies that extends beyond retail, animating its relationship to other sectors of the economy and other kinds of economic transaction.

In so doing, there is also an opportunity to extend the emerging expectation that high streets must make a 'more-than-economic' contribution to local communities, to posit other ways of measuring that contribution beyond traditional indicators such as GDP, and ultimately to displace the "imagined autonomy of the economy" (Clarke 30). In relation to this challenge, the dénouement of Melvin's picture book presents a timely reminder of the interconnectedness of the high street and local public infrastructure, and of the fact that shared experiences of collective goods – such as memories of yellow roses admired in a public park – can be much more valuable than private acquisition.

Third, my analysis of the idealised high street underscores the necessity of interrogating the role of nostalgia in contemporary economic imaginaries. The idealised high street sustains both reactionary and radical visions of national identity and of the role of the economy in a future society. Both have a nostalgic dimension, and so it is vital to scrutinise the ways in which nostalgia for former modes of economic organisation can naturalise exclusions on the basis of race or class. As my discussion of the Waltham Forest planning guidance makes clear, an understanding of the built environment of the high street as 'heritage' can certainly be used to reinforce such exclusions. Yet, if we look beyond this overly-thematised issue, and if we take a cue from Griffiths's emphasis on the "historical potential of the high street to generate patterns of social co-presence, encounter and engagement" (41), this functional and symbolic site can be understood to harbour 'historical' resources that are potentially far more disruptive and challenging. For example, high streets are sites where the exclusions and divisions of the past (Watson and Wells) might in fact be reactivated and traced through to the present moment. The incorporation of the desires and investments of socially and economically marginalised subjects for their local high streets and communities could activate their potential to deliver meaningful "cross-cultural contact and related economic experimentation" (Hall 2573).

CONCLUSION

The idealised high street is a compromised site of meaning in which diverse hopes and desires for a shared economic future are invested. This means that it is open to contestation. It can be articulated to progressive politics – to Labour's institutional turn, for example – but it can also be articulated to reactionary, protectionist and ultimately racist visions of Britain's future. If we are to achieve 'economic system change', it will be necessary to foster economic imaginaries that sustain such a transformation. The extension of democracy into economic life will necessitate meaningful critical scrutiny and redress of the ways in which economic imaginaries sustain deep exclusions. The idealised high street is a cornerstone of contemporary economic imaginaries and it will remain a space that opens up opportunities to envision and enact social, political, and economic change.

REFERENCES

Alakeson, Vidhya. "High Streets Can Be Saved. Here's How to Reinvent them for the 21st Century." *The Guardian*, 1 May 2019, www.theguardian.com/commentisfree/2019/may/01/high-streets-saved-debenhams-close-stores.

Anderson, Ben, and Helen F. Wilson. "Everyday Brexits." *Area,* vol. 50, no. 2, 2018, pp. 291-95.

Benson, John, and Laura Ugolini. "Introduction: Historians and the Nation of Shopkeepers." *A Nation of Shopkeepers: Five Centuries of British Retailing,* edited by John Benson and Laura Ugolini, I.B. Tauris, 2003, pp. 1-24.

Birch, Kean. "Emergent Imaginaries and Fragmented Policy Frameworks in the Canadian Bio-Economy." *Sustainability,* vol. 8, no. 10, 2016, pp. 1007-16.

Bramall, Rebecca. *The Cultural Politics of Austerity: Past and Present in Austere Times.* Palgrave Macmillan, 2013.

Clarke, John. "Imagined Economies: Austerity and the Moral Economy of 'Fairness.'" *Topia: Canadian Journal of Cultural Studies,* vol. 30-31, 2013, pp. 17-30.

Clements Hall Local History Group. *Bishy Road: A York Shopping Street in Time.* Clements Hall, 2018.

Dominiczak, Peter. "Britain to Become a "Nation of Shopkeepers Again", Ministers Pledge." *Telegraph,* 10 August 2015, www.telegraph.co.uk/news/politics/conservative/11795160/Britain-to-become-a-nation-of-shopkeepers-again-ministers-pledge.html.

Fletcher, Gordon, et al. "Creatively Prototyping the Future High Street." *Production Planning & Control,* vol. 27, no. 6, 2016, pp. 477-89.

Griffiths, Sam. "The High Street as Morphological Event." *Suburban Urbanities,* edited by Laura Vaughan, UCL Press, 2015, pp. 32-52.

Guinan, Joe, and Martin O'Neill. "From Community Wealth Building to System Change: Local Roots for Economic Transformation." *IPPR Progressive Review,* vol. 25, no. 4, 2019, pp. 382-92.

—, and O'Neill, M. "The Institutional Turn: Labour's New Political Economy." *Renewal,* vol. 26, no. 2, 2018, pp. 5-16.

Hall, Suzanne. "High Street Adaptations: Ethnicity, Independent Retail Practices, and Localism in London's Urban Margins." *Environment and Planning A: Economy and Space,* vol. 43, no. 11, 2011, pp. 2571-88.

Hanna, Thomas, et al. "The 'Preston Model' and the Modern Politics of Municipal Socialism." *openDemocracy,* 12 June 2018, neweconomics.opendemocracy.net/preston-model-modern-politics-municipal-socialism/.

Harris, John. "Rebuild the Faded Towns of Britain to End our National Malaise." *The Guardian,* 4 February 2019, www.theguardian.com/commentisfree/2019/feb/04/rebuild-faded-towns-britain.

Hatherley, Owen. "London Streets Don't Need to Look Like a 1940s that Never Happened." *Dezeen*, 7 November 2017, www.dezeen. com/2017/11/07/owen-hatherley-opinion-walthamstow-high-street-london-shop-signs-sanitisation-mistake/.

Haywood, Jo. "What Makes York's Bishopthorpe Road so Special?" *Yorkshire Life*, 13 February 2017, www.yorkshirelife.co.uk/out-ab out/places/what-makes-york-s-bishopthorpe-road-so-special-1-488 5228.

Hewison, Robert. *The Heritage Industry: Britain in a Climate of Decline*. Methuen, 1987

Hubbard, Philip. "Enthusiasm, Craft and Authenticity on the High Street: Micropubs as 'Community Fixers.'" *Social & Cultural Geography,* vol. 20, no. 6, 2019, pp. 763-84.

Jessop, Bob. "Cultural Political Economy and Critical Policy Studies." *Critical Policy Studies,* vol. 3, no. 3-4, 2010, pp. 336-56.

Lekakis, Eleftheria. "Economic Nationalism and the Cultural Politics of Consumption under Austerity." *Journal of Consumer Culture,* vol. 17, no. 2, 2017, pp. 286-302.

London Borough of Waltham Forest. *Shop Front Design Supplementary Planning Document*. 2016, www.walthamforest.gov.uk.

Marsh, Alec. "Crumbling Britain: The Slow Death of the High Street." *New Statesman*, 11 July 2018, www.newstatesman.com/politics/uk/ 2018/07/crumbling-britain-slow-death-high-street.

McDonald, Ojay, and Kim Cassidy. "Guest Editorial." *Journal of Place Management and Development,* vol. 10, no. 4, 2017, pp. 307-09.

Meek, James. *Dreams of Leaving and Remaining*. Verso, 2019.

Melvin, Alice. *The High Street*. Tate Publishing, 2011.

Morrison, Caitlin. "UK Retail Sales Show Biggest Decline in 23 Years." *Independent*, 9 May 2018, www.independent.co.uk/news/business/ news/uk-retail-sales-drop-consumer-spending-austerity-wages-inco me-brc-a8342661.html.

Portas, Mary. "The Portas Review: An Independent Review Into the Future of our High Streets." *Gov.uk*, 2011, www.gov.uk/government/ publications/the-portas-review-the-future-of-our-high-streets.

Ray, Larry, and Andrew Sayer. "Introduction." *Culture and Economy after the Cultural Turn,* edited by Larry Ray and Andrew Sayer, Sage, 1999, pp. 1-24.

Rushby, Kevin. "'It Could be Terrible for Us': How One British High Street is Preparing for Brexit." *The Guardian,* 19 March 2019, www.theguardian.com/lifeandstyle/2019/mar/19/brexit-bishy-road-bishopthorpe-york-high-streets-survive-shopkeepers.

—. "How to Bring a High Street Back from the Dead." *The Guardian,* 29 March 2018, www.theguardian.com/lifeandstyle/2018/mar/29/high-street-closed-betting-shops-york-back-from-dead.

Samuel, Raphael. *Theatres of Memory.* Verso, 1994.

Sayid, Ruki. "Waterstones under Fire for Opening Stores on the High Street Disguised as Independent Book Shops." *Mirror,* 27 February 2017, www.mirror.co.uk/news/uk-news/waterstones-under-fire-opening-stores-9928822.

Sikka, Prem. "Here's How to Save the High Street." *Left Foot Forward,* 28 March 2019, leftfootforward.org/2019/03/prem-sikka-heres-how-to-save-the-high-street/.

Swartz, Lana. "What Was Bitcoin, What Will it be? The Techno-Economic Imaginaries of a New Money Technology." *Cultural Studies,* vol. 32, no. 4, 2018, pp. 623-50.

Virdee, Satnam, and Brendan McGeever. "Racism, Crisis, Brexit." *Ethnic and Racial Studies,* vol. 41, no. 10, 2018, pp. 1802-19.

Watson, Sophie, and Karen Wells. "Spaces of Nostalgia: the Hollowing out of a London Market." *Social & Cultural Geography,* vol. 6, no. 1, 2005, pp. 17-30.

Weldon, Duncan. "The British Model and the Brexit Shock: Plus Ça Change?" *Political Quarterly,* vol. 90, no. 2, 2019, pp. 12-20.

Wright, Patrick. *On Living In An Old Country – The National Past in Contemporary Britain.* Verso, 1985.

The New Democratic Economy:
An Imaginary and Real Alternative

Luke Martell

An alternative economy is being built in the UK and beyond. It comes out of radical imagination, yet is material and real and draws on but breaks with previous paradigms. It is complex, detailed and practical, based in pluralities, governmental and civil society, political and economic, and in its regenerative capacities can appeal across the political spectrum. People are talking about it and doing it, from local governments, to think tanks, academics, and national political parties, moving beyond globalisation and neoliberalism. But can something localised avoid parochialism and competition, represent the interests of the public as a whole and work nationally and beyond? Will the alternative economy's embeddedness across institutions and via plural actors protect it from reversal? Can the democratic economy survive as an imagine-and-do, not just imagining, approach?

LABOUR, CONSERVATIVES AND SOCIAL OWNERSHIP

In 1945, the Labour Party came to power in the UK, nationalised major industries and established the National Health Service (NHS). 34 years later Margaret Thatcher became Prime Minister and instigated widespread privatisation of state assets. This direction of policy continued under Tony Blair, who removed the commitment to public ownership from the Labour Party constitution. The private sector and market became default policy choices, until the 2015 victory of Jeremy Corbyn as Labour leader brought back the value of public ownership as mainstream rather than marginal. Socialism and social democracy have long espoused social ownership of production and greater equality in the distribution of income and services. Corbyn's proposals see these as linked. Rather than allowing inequality to grow and be equalised through redistribution, ownership of assets is seen as key to equality of wealth and income (Guinan and O'Neill, "The Institutional Turn").

Labour's manifesto for the 2017 general election proposed socially owned local energy companies as alternatives to big corporate providers, and the nationalisation of energy, water and the Royal Mail. Labour argue for insourcing council services, municipal social ownership, assistance for the growth of the co-operative sector and transferring company shares to workers. The emphasis is on decentralised social ownership; and when national ownership then in a democratised form. A report for the party on alternative models of ownership discusses co-ops, municipal and national state ownership, community wealth building, procurement by anchor institutions and the model of local economic regeneration practiced by Preston's Labour Council (Labour Party, *For the Many*; *Alternative Models*).

What I am considering in this chapter, though, are not only party policies. Proposals for social ownership and local wealth building are also being discussed by think tanks like The Democracy Collaborative in the USA and the UK Centre for Local Economic Strategy (CLES).

These do not just produce policy but are hands-on and guide implementation. Much talked about sites for carrying out social ownership policies, with the assistance of such think-and-do tanks, are in Cleveland, Ohio in the USA and Preston in the UK. Key principles in such approaches are: community and collaboration, place and locality, democratic ownership and systemic and institutional change, inclusion, good work and the workforce, multiplier effects, and sustainability and ethical finance (Kelly et al.; Kelly and Howard).

COMMUNITY WEALTH BUILDING: FROM AN EXTRACTIVE TO A CIRCULATORY ECONOMY

These initiatives involve community wealth building, where wealth is generated and retained locally, with political intervention to support socially owned business and build links between community business and anchor institutions in communities (Kelly et al.; Brown et al.; Guinan and O'Neill, *The Case for Community*). Anchor institutions are those like hospitals, universities or councils more or less tied to the locality. They can be encouraged to shift the outsourcing of services from large corporations to local, sometimes socially owned, providers. The result is that, rather than flowing away to big corporations and their shareholders, money is kept in the community.

Proponents say this moves away from an extractive economy, where money is taken out of localities by capitalist corporations, to a circulatory one, where it stays in the locality. For Matthew Brown, leader of Preston City Council, it is about creating an alternative economic system at a local level (Brown and O'Neill). Brown et al. argue that finance focuses on property and land instead of employment-rich investments in manufacturing and services, and that investment in automation leads to wealth being held less by society in the form of jobs and more by capital extracted by investors (Brown et al. 134; Labour Party, *Alternative Models*).[1] Retaining money locally, however, can help generate work in the community. The approach is also a method of responding to local government cuts by looking at remaining wealth in the community and trying to keep it there. Furthermore, by the economy being tied increasingly to the locality, rather than to international investors, it is more insulated from global economic shocks like the financial crisis (Brown and O'Neill 73). There is an equality element because wealth is captured for workers, community owners and reinvestment, instead of being allowed to disappear away to capital and shareholders. In this sense community wealth-building is not just a technical approach for fostering local economies but also about power, re-balancing it away from international capital to local more democratic entities, such as government-owned or socially owned enterprises (O'Neill and Howard 52).

These approaches fit with a trend towards remunicipalisation wherein services are returned to the local public sector, reversing outsourcing and replacing privatisation and the public-private partnerships favoured by New Labour (Kishimoto et al.). Preston Council's assessment is that between 2012/13 and 2016/17 procurement spend retained in the city rose from £38.3m (5%) to £112.3m (18.2%), and within surrounding Lancashire from £288.7m (18.2%) to £488.7m (79.2%), despite declining overall by 15%. 4,000 extra employees are receiving the 'living wage', and Preston has won awards for its improvement on various social and economic indicators, moved up its position on an index of social mobility, been lifted out of the 20% most deprived areas in the UK, and unemployment has dropped below the national average (CLES and Preston City Council 12-13, 20-21).

---

1   Alternative Models of Ownership focuses on social ownership of automation
    to make sure the benefits go to workers and society.

INSTITUTIONAL, OWNERSHIP AND SYSTEM CHANGE: A ROAD TO SOCIALISM?

For Guinan and O'Neill, Corbyn's approach involves an institutional turn, democratic economy proposals being focused on structure, design and system, a predistribution and asset-based more than redistributional approach to equality (Guinan and O'Neill, "The Institutional Turn"). Rather than income inequalities growing and being corrected, a more equal ownership of assets and equitable distribution is encouraged from the start. Equality is pursued through social ownership of wealth and relations between community institutions instead of the focus being on income distribution. This involves a shift of power as well as income because ordinary people are empowered in ownership which is not always the case in social democratic redistribution.

Part of the case for this approach is on democratic grounds, that we do not have democracy unless it is widened to the economy as well as politics, and that political democracy is undermined if economic power can shape political decisions thereby reducing accountability of politicians to citizens who voted for them (Beckett; Guinan and O'Neill, *From Community Wealth*; Labour Party, *Alternative Models*; New Socialist). The democracy envisaged is often quite participatory, with people playing a greater role in the governance of businesses and utilities, especially where decentralised. A question this raises is whether there is enough of a participatory consciousness in society for this to work. Insofar as participation happens it may be biased to those with agency, time and money (Heslop et al. 11). The pressure group We Own It argue that people will participate if they have the chance to in an inspiring way (We Own It 9; Guinan and O'Neill, *From Community Wealth*). But there have been problems motivating, for example, parents and members of the community to be involved in school governance; and offering meaningful participation in co-ops does not necessarily lead to it being taken up (Carter 8, 3). Democratic participation may need more than structures, but also a change in consciousness, a cultural and not just a political shift. This involves constructing a narrative and discourse about participation that links to people's real lives and interests and mobilises them behind its material structure, a hegemonic strategy (Hall).[2]

Are democratic economy proposals socialist and intended to replace capitalism or are they social democratic and aiming for change within the boundaries of capitalism? They are not in themselves an approach to overthrow capitalism, at least not yet, so in that sense are social democratic as much as socialist (Brown et al. describe it as social democratic, 134-5). Reducing the contracting of international capitalist companies in favour of local community procurement does not go after capital so much as sidestep or exclude it to favour local wealth and to parallel social ownership. It competes with international capital rather than nationalising capital and creates democratic capital more than democratising existing capital.

But the democratic economy reduces the role of international capital, builds social ownership and tries to direct investment to social ends. It involves systemic change to wider public local forms. Asking whether these proposals are about either changing capitalism or abolishing it is too binary a question because while they live with capitalism, they also reduce it by building non-capitalist forms. They are about replacing international corporate control where possible with local, socially owned democracy. Hence Guinan and O'Neill see Corbyn's proposals as socialist (Guinan and O'Neill, "The Institutional Turn"; Guinan and Hanna; New Socialist 109, 113; Labour Party, *Alternative Models* 32). The democratic economy is more structural than redistributional and involves a shift in power and equality through social ownership, as in socialist perspectives, as opposed to after the fact redistribution and regulations of a social democratic kind. These accept a privately owned capitalist economy but try to control and correct for its maldistributions.

---

2   This was advocated by Stuart Hall, drawing on Gramsci, in relation to the left in the Thatcher period.

Beckett, however, asks whether the regeneration of local economies by community wealth building helps save capitalism in a moderated, diluted, pluralised form that allows it to regroup and come back more red in tooth and claw (Beckett). This is a significant point, however, local democratic economy proposals can, and do in Labour Party policy, combine with the nationalisation of privately owned companies and so complement a politics that does not just dilute capitalism but also takes it over collectively.

PLURALITY OF INSTITUTIONS: COMPLEXITY AND REVERSIBILITY

The democratic economy involves a plurality of institutions: socially owned enterprises of various sorts, community or government created, with local and national government input to support social ownership and build relations between them and anchor institutions. Government can facilitate leadership, tax breaks, loans, investment, procurement, and shelter organisations that fund, promote and support social ownership. There are the anchor institutions themselves and their local procurement policy. Then think tanks are involved as in Preston and Cleveland. Institutions in proposals also include municipal enterprise, land trusts, public trusts, public banks and participatory budgeting. Initiatives may rise out of social movements and support comes also from philanthropy and trade unions. This departs from narrower approaches based on, say, government action or anti-political alternatives. More social agents and institutions are involved which makes the restructured economy more complex as well as making it more systemic and institutional.

One aim is that such institutional interrelatedness makes democratic economy systems difficult to dismantle in the way nationalised industry and utilities were in the UK. Embedding change in society, it is hoped, is more likely to outlast changes of government and reversals by subsequent unsympathetic politicians. For Beckett, democratic economy proposals are for something more systemic and permanent than nationalisation and tax (Beckett). If less centrally linked to the state, as tax and nationalisation are, then it is more difficult for a change of government to reverse them.[3] This also comes from plurality of forms of ownership, actors and approaches and from potential attractiveness across the political spectrum.

However, publicly owned companies could be sold, and local and municipal social ownership and procurement policy can be blocked or reversed by competition regulation or changes in political control of a local council or national government. The new democratic economy would be more complex to unravel than nationalisations or regulations but this would still be possible for a new government willing to change policy and dismantle relations and support. The question of reversibility is not clearly answered by appeals to the changes as systemic and institutionalised because systems and institutions can be politically changed. Furthermore, the case is often focused on changes of government rolling back democratic economic systems, an answer being that subsequent administrations may like the local regenerative effects of circulatory community wealth building and so keep it. But key actors who are disadvantaged are international capital. Even if the local economy stays capitalist and for-profit, global capital still gets increasingly sidelined. The latter may be as much a threat to the circulatory economy, and its economic power as much a challenge as political changes of government. Faced with global corporate opposition political governments might become less supportive of local wealth retention.

So, community wealth building may need a strategy beyond systemic embeddedness for maintaining its initiatives. It might need to include a basis in social movements and popular consciousness as well as in institutions and political and economic systems. The editors of New Socialist emphasise the importance of values, culture and movements in supporting democratic economy changes in the face of opposition from

---

3   Wainwright (27) and We Own It (9 and 38) argue for institutionalising to make it difficult for public services to be dismantled in the future.

international capital, from inside government institutions, like the civil service, and from within the Labour Party (New Socialist). They argue that culture and socialisation are as important as economic control and planning. New Socialist also mention values like co-operation, solidarity, empathy and charity as important bedrocks for the democratic economy. They argue that democratic structures are important not just in themselves but for bringing in and sustaining support for that which is democratised. However, it will take more than structures to build culture and values that help the democratic economy work and protect it from the threat of reversal discussed in this chapter.

SOCIAL CHANGE AND SCALING UP

One question is whether experiments like Preston and Cleveland can be widened and scaled up to large scale transformation. Local approaches can be experimental, testing to see whether the idea works; if it does, then they can be demonstrative to others that the idea works and how. There is a prefigurative element (see Wainwright), building alternatives within capitalism, but as a basis for a wider non-capitalist economy along the same lines. Initiatives like those in Preston can and do grow into good practice spreading across local authorities (see Leibowitz and McInroy). That such approaches are in Labour's manifesto is a sign of examples like Preston widening outwards and rising upwards. Furthermore, the democratic economy can develop, not only by showing things can work through experiment and demonstration, encouraging adoption and scaling up from below, but also through political leadership at government level and through mainstream public sector anchor institutions.[4] The Preston Model is more in mainstream society than on its margins or in separate spaces; it is more in politics and public-public relationships than other social alternatives, so less outside politics; and it is open to

---

4   Creating what Common Wealth call public-commons partnerships: see Milburn and Russell.

being developed and scaled up by means additional to prefiguration, through a political and not just a social basis for change.

Cumbers and Hanna discuss the role of government in scaling up local initiatives (Cumbers and Hanna 18ff.). Government can pursue change through: top-down nationalisations and remunicipalisation; tax and funding support for social ownership and allowing first refusal for employees to buy companies at risk of closure or takeover; and public procurement policies that favour co-ops and social and environmental goals. A number of these are Labour policies under Corbyn. This is built on on-the-ground experimentation to be promoted at national level by government. A community wealth building unit being established in Corbyn's office shows the potential for the approach nationally.[5] Democratic economy proposals in Labour's 2017 manifesto and its report on *Alternative Models of Ownership* have been important in re-incorporating public ownership on to the national agenda even if Labour do not come to power.[6]

As the approaches discussed involve funds being reinvested locally, rather than leaving the area, they may also appeal to Conservatives concerned with local economic regeneration, although we shall see that from another perspective this is problematic.[7] New Socialist argue that Labour's policies have a 'sober practicality' to them and can appeal to the right (New Socialist). They do not necessarily involve higher tax or public spending or nationalisation which could be off-putting from a

---

5 Howard's speech at the launch of Corbyn's community wealth unit ("The Democracy Collaborative") discusses widening out and scaling up of the approach as do Guinan and O'Neill in "The Institutional Turn". Beckett also charts such policies taking form in the hands of John McDonnell and the Labour leadership.

6 See Hanna, "The Next Economic", and Guinan and Hanna on how public ownership is back for the Labour Party and back on the agenda more generally.

7 See O'Neill and Howard, 46-7, on the argument that community wealth building can appeal across the political spectrum.

right-wing perspective. This makes them easier to spread, implement and sustain across changes in government. However, the appeal may only be to those on the right that value place-based wealth building and local economic development. Conservatives in class terms, as representatives of international capital, will be less convinced as global capital is undermined by this approach in which it loses contracts to local contractors. Many on the right will be put off by some of this as being overly co-operative, non-capitalist enterprise, eroding the place of private capital and seen by them as less efficient.

LOCALISM AND ITS LIMITS? COMMUNITY, COMPETITION AND INEQUALITY

There may be limits in the localism of democratic economy proposals. They might be suited to areas with local identity, attachment to place and place-based entities that can be anchor institutions, but less viable in areas lacking these.[8] Retention of wealth by the community rather than extraction by corporate capital will be welcomed by most with left-wing and community concerns. More contentious may be its retention locally at the expense of the community beyond. Proposals can be seen to be concerned with local interests, and so parochial and insular, and not with the interests and welfare of the wider community nationally and globally. It is about fostering local interests potentially to the disadvantage of other localities.

For poor areas retaining wealth for local regeneration may make sense. But as a policy implemented more widely localism could mean wealth is retained in better off areas when its spread to poorer communities would be desirable. One solution is pursuing the approach within a more redistributive approach at national or supra-national levels. So, in areas where wealth builds up some of it could be redistributed to

---

8   Heslop et al., 9, on Swansea. Brown says Preston is lucky with its anchor institutions, see Brown and O'Neill.

poorer places. This requires local wealth generators not losing the incentive to create and retain wealth locally if they know some will be redistributed away. However, this does not mean it is not do-able or done already under existing redistributive structures.

Ted Howard of The Democracy Collaborative rejects the 'beggar thy neighbour' criticism for this stage of spreading community wealth building which he says is about resetting the balance between local communities and international capital, as much as localities versus localities (O'Neill and Howard 49-50). O'Neill argues that local government has to promote local economic development in the absence of other approaches and given national government's lack of commitment to reducing inequality. Furthermore, what the community wealth approach replaces is, for Howard, itself protectionism where cities compete to attract investment at the expense of other cities (O'Neill and Howard 49-50). The difference from community wealth building is that this allows profits to go out of the area to international shareholders not committed in an ongoing way to the local community.

O'Neill suggests there are two paths: one is favouring local institutions and the other those with more ethical standards (Brown and O'Neill). The two can go together but the emphasis on ethical and social business implies supporting alternative economic structures as much as, or sometimes rather than, local regeneration. Favouring social business over local business where the two do not coincide is hard for a local authority but gives an ethical rather than localist slant to the approach. Preston Council say choosing suppliers based on social value has not always meant the local one. Furthermore, the Preston policy led to a shift in contracts away from London and the south-east, but not from the rest of the country, so did not mean abandoning a commitment to a wider community beyond the local one (CLES and Preston City Council 23).

A related issue is that the community wealth approach can lead to competition and inequality. In locally focused wealth creation and retention approaches areas may be focused on their interests and become competitive with other areas, and in competition there are winners and

losers, so inequalities grow. Competition can lead to wasteful duplica-
tion, and reluctance to share resources or information, such as research
and design. This can be the case with local authorities or local co-ops
competing. Hanna says competition and whether this is a good thing is
an issue as much as ownership is (Hanna, "The Next Economic" 22). A
further dimension is that co-ops run the risk of being as biased to the
sectional group that owns them, for instance workers, as localism can be
to the locality. Wider forms of ownership can help to counter sectionalism and competitive inequality that arises from specific ownership or
localism.

NATIONAL AND PUBLIC OWNERSHIP

National forms of public ownership may be desirable, so there is less
replication of activities and more sharing of information than under decentralised forms (see Hanna, "The Next Economic"; *Our Common
Wealth*). This need not replace local ownership. Pluralism is desirable
for various reasons, and in many cases local accountability and participation is positive. Another possible approach is networks between co-
ops and local authorities with agreements not to compete or conceal resources and information.

Hobbs argues that public ownership represents the public as a whole
and all those affected by a company's actions, not just particular groups
(such as workers in worker's co-ops) or communities (as in localism).
Similarly, for Cumbers and Hanna municipal ownership is better than
other local forms because it covers all groups in the area. Public ownership can overcome insularity and sectionalism and oversee equality between areas, so some do not grow better off at the expense of others.
New Socialist editors argue public ownership can also ensure greater
equality of service nationally. A further question, that there is not space
to discuss here, concerns the development of equality internationally.

For Hobbs and We Own It we should not denigrate state ownership
too much. It has been equated too easily with centralised, bureaucratic,

inefficient, top-down organisation, despite evidence of efficiency (Hobbs 42; We Own It; Cumbers and Hanna 9). State ownership has worked for rail in other European countries and for the NHS, for example, and beyond the UK it is widespread, even in the free market USA (Hanna, *Our Common Wealth*; "The Next Economic"; Guinan and Hanna 118ff.). It allows economies of scale, consistency, equality and cross-subsidy (Hobbs; New Socialist; We Own It; Cumbers and Hanna). Furthermore, more sectional groups face greater market pressures so may externalise environmental costs (Cumbers and Hanna 12, 15-16). State ownership can be better on environmental grounds. Because of its scale it can have a large impact if pursuing green policies.[9]

The Legatum Institute found that three quarters of the UK public, with support across generations and party allegiance, believe water, electricity, gas and rail should be publicly owned, and 50% feel the banks should be nationalised (Elliott and Kanagasooriam 14-17). A YouGov poll shows lower but still majority support for nationalisation of Royal Mail, water, rail, and energy, across age, class and region (Smith). Labour's report on alternative models discusses national ownership and arguments for it, acknowledging its pitfalls and the case for democratisation through the inclusion of involved and affected groups in governance: local and national states, workers, consumers, managers, experts and community groups (Labour Party, *Alternative Models* 27-31; see also We Own It). Public ownership may need to be reformed from forms it has taken in the past. Its problems, such as they have been, could be addressed by investigating forms of management as much as by a shift to private ownership. Reform of public ownership can involve both democratising it and reforming management and these may be related and go hand in hand.

---

9   For New Socialist national public ownership is the level at which to tackle issues like climate change.

THE IMAGINARY AND REAL ALTERNATIVE

How is the economy imagined in democratic economy proposals? It is about local value, economic and social, not international corporate value, the creation and retention of wealth in the community rather than extracting it from outside for shareholders over citizens. It involves institutionalisation of the alternative and change through a system and assets, rather than leaving these and compensating by redistributional correction. The democratic economy is pluralist. It marries political and civil society, the mainstream and the margins. There is a politicisation of alternatives, social alternatives built on and linked with political intervention, a role for the entrepreneurial state, local and national, instead of rejection of active government, in alliance with various institutions including the mainstream public sector. It involves alternatives, not in isolated experiments on the fringes of society, but through conventional politics, set up downwards and scaled across as well as scaled up from below.

The democratic economy is perhaps not socialism replacing social democracy, but rather socialist as well as social democratic. It is more Old Labour than New Labour but with a greater role for the local and decentralised. Local reinvestment can also appeal to local communities and non-socialists. This is part of its practical edge, although it may encourage parochial self-interest. The democratic economy is imaginary but also real, involving think-and-do action and not just thinking. For Howard it is a materially emerging economy, rather than theoretical (Howard, "The Making of"). For Guinan and Hanna it is not a fantasy but involves real-world alternative democratic economy institutions internationally, some charted by them (Guinan and Hanna 110, 114ff.).

A question with alternatives is how they can be realised, entrenched and institutionalised. Can the democratic economy have appeal beyond the left, be ingrained to resist reversal and can it challenge capitalism as opposed to diluting it? The democratic economy involves the materialisation, politicisation and pluralisation, through institutions and broad support, of an alternative economy. Its potential for scaling up is being realised. But even if the political right can be convinced, this economy will face opposition from international capital as it would find itself at a disadvantage. Complacency over parochialism, resistance and the potential for reversal needs to be avoided. To ensure embeddedness in society in the face of opposition from global capital, there will need to be a popular consciousness and social movement basis behind the democratic economy, as well as institutionalisation.

REFERENCES

Beckett, Andy. "The New Left Economics: How a Network of Thinkers is Transforming Capitalism." *The Guardian*, 25 June 2019.

Brown, Matthew, Ted Howard, Matthew Jackson, and Neil McInroy. "A New Urban System: the UK and the US." *Economics for the Many*, edited by John McDonnell, Verso, 2018.

—, and Martin O'Neill. "The Road to Socialism is the A59: The Preston Model." *Renewal*, vol. 24, no. 2, 2016.

Carter, Neil. "Political Participation and the Workplace: The Spillover Thesis Revisited." *British Journal of Politics and International Relations*, vol. 8, no. 3, 2006.

CLES and Preston City Council. *How We Built Community Wealth in Preston: Achievements and Lessons*. Preston City Council, 2019.

Cumbers, Andrew, and Thomas Hanna. "Democratic Ownership." *New Thinking for the British Economy*, edited by Laurie Macfarlane, Open Democracy, 2018.

Elliott, Matthew, and James Kanagasooriam. *Public Opinion in the Post-Brexit Era: Economic Attitudes in Modern Britain*. Legatum Institute, 2017.

Guinan, Joe, and Thomas Hanna. "Democratic Ownership in the New Economy." *Economics for the Many*, edited by John McDonnell, Verso, 2018.

—, and Martin O'Neill. *From Community Wealth Building to System Change: Local Roots for Economic Transformation*. IPPR, 2019.

—, and Martin O'Neill. *The Case for Community Wealth Building*. Polity Press, 2019.

—, and Martin O'Neill. "The Institutional Turn: Labour's New Political Economy." *Renewal*, vol. 26, no. 2, 2018.

Hall, Stuart. *The Hard Road to Renewal: Thatcherism and the Crisis of the Left*. Verso, 1988.

Hanna, Thomas. *Our Common Wealth: The Return of Public Ownership in the United States*. Manchester University Press, 2018.

—. "The Next Economic Settlement: The Return of Public Ownership." *Renewal*, vol. 26, no. 2, 2018.

Heslop, Julia, Kevin Morgan, and John Tomaney. "Debating the Foundational Economy." *Renewal,* vol. 27, no. 2, 2019.

Hobbs, Cat. "Doing Public Ownership: Centralisation, Decentralisation, Bureaucracy and Control." *Renewal*, vol. 26, no. 3, 2018.

Howard, Ted. "The Democracy Collaborative Joins Jeremy Corbyn's New Community Wealth Building Unit as Advisors." *The Democracy Collaborative*, 8 February 2018.

—. "The Making of a Democratic Economy." *RSA*, 2018, www.thersa.org/events/2018/11/the-making-of-a-democratic-economy.

Kelly, Marjorie, and Ted Howard. *The Making of a Democratic Economy: How to Build Prosperity for the Many, Not the Few*. Berrett-Koehler Publishers, 2019.

—, Sarah McKinley, and Violeta Duncan. "Politics of Place/Politics for Places: Community Wealth Building: America's Emerging Asset-Based Approach to City Economic Development." *Renewal*, vol. 24, no. 2, 2015.

Kishimoto, Satoko, Olivier Petitjean, and Lavinia Steinfort. *Reclaiming Public Services: How Cities and Citizens are Turning back Privatisation*. TNI, 2017.

Labour Party. *Alternative Models of Ownership*. Labour Party, 2017.

—. *For the Many Not the Few: The Labour Party Manifesto 2017*. Labour Party, 2017.

Leibowitz, Jonty, and Neil McInroy. "Beyond Preston: How Local Wealth Building is Taking the UK by Storm." *CityMetric*, 25 March 2019.

McDonnell, John. *Economics for the Many*. Verso, 2018.

Milburn, Keir, and Bertie Russell. "Public-Common Partnerships: Building New Circuits of Collective Ownership." *Common Wealth*, 27 June 2019.

New Socialist. "Labour's Alternative Models of Ownership Report." *New Socialist*, 11 June 2017.

O'Neill, Martin, and Ted Howard. "Beyond Extraction: The Political Power of Community Wealth Building." *Renewal*, vol. 26, no. 2, 2018.

Smith, Matthew. "Nationalisation vs Privatisation: The Public View." *YouGov*, 19 May 2017.

Wainwright, Hilary. "Creating an Economy that Works for All." *For the Many: Preparing Labour for Power*, edited by Mike Phipps, OR Books, 2017.

We Own It. *When We Own It: A Model for Public Ownership in the 21st Century*. We Own It, 2019.

Imaginary Economies:
Narratives for the 21st Century

Melissa Kennedy

In Aesop's famous fable, "The Ant and the Grasshopper," first told about 2,500 years ago, the fun-loving grasshopper sings all summer while the industrious ant puts away stores for winter. When winter comes, the starving grasshopper begs the ant for food. The ant refuses, and the story stops there, leaving the reader to assume that the grasshopper dies of hunger. The moral of the story, often written at the bottom of the page in print editions, is the importance of saving now in order to put something away for hard times later. As literature, Aesop's fable gives a uniquely literary perspective on old economic arguments, an ancient reminder of how the economy is always storied into being. The tale follows a narrative arc, complete with dramatic tension and closure at the end. The third-person narrative viewpoint gives equal agency to the two characters that both tell the reader how they think and feel. Having given us both sides of the story, Aesop's fable puts readers in a difficult position, asking us first to identify and empathise with both characters, then forcing us to choose our allegiance to one at the expense of the other: should the cheerful grasshopper die or should we recognise the hard work and foresight (with embedded ideas of ambition, good upbringing and seeming intelligence) of the ant? Faced with this moral dilemma, the easiest reader response is to close the book, relieved that this story is only fiction. We might further suspect that the story's sketchy, obscure, inconclusive message illustrates the restricted usefulness of art to interpreting the real world we live in: luckily we are not often confronted with making such moral judgements and decisions as the ant in the story does.

Aesop's parable illustrates one aspect of what we might call "imaginary economics": it is a story, the function of which is to convey an economic narrative. Encoded in it are certain mechanisms of abundance and scarcity, supply and demand, saving and expenditure, the value of labour and cultural work, independence and trust, and of potential reciprocal trading arrangements – here foreclosed by the selfish ant. As a parable, it has a socio-cultural function telling us how the world works. It suggests that life is unfair; that nothing grows in winter; that one can't rely on a neighbour to help; and it even contains speciest or racist overtones that a certain ethnicity is attractive but lazy and another is hardworking and deserving. Like all good fairy tales, it is a warning contained in a threat.

Certainly, there are many ways to read the fable, depending on both historical and individual perspectives and values. Over its 2,500-year life, the simple story has been interpreted differently according to changing value systems. This chapter uses "The Ant and the Grasshopper" to illustrate the usefulness of bringing together two disciplines commonly held apart: the social science of economics and the humanities field of literary and cultural studies. As economics is a narrative of human interaction, invented and imagined into being with the help of figurative language and dominant story tropes, literary studies' interpretative and critical approaches open new ways of framing and engaging with economic criticism. Thus, I argue that the dominant interpretation of Aesop's fable reflects contemporary critiques of both the justice and the sustainability of neoliberal free-market global capitalism. In the spirit of recent calls by economists to rethink the dominant narratives of economics, I end by proposing a rereading and rewriting of "The Ant and the Grasshopper" to fit the 21st century shift to an ethical, sustainable economic narrative.

There are several grounds on which to claim that the disciplines of literature and economics are closely related. The historical roots of classical economics lie in ethics and philosophy. Before they were labelled the fathers of economics, John Locke, David Hume, and Adam Smith were known for their considerations of human well-being within the Greco-Roman philosophical tradition of virtue ethics. Locke's *An Essay Concerning Human Understanding* (1689), Hume's *An Enquiry Concerning the Principles of Morals* (1751) and Smith's *Theory of Moral Sentiments* (1759) are no longer widely read. Instead, aspects of their work that have become keystones of classical economics misrepresent their writers' beliefs. These include: Locke on private property, misattributed in the US Declaration of Independence; Hume's form of early utilitarianism, applied in social policy by Jeremy Bentham and John Stuart Mill; and Smith's much misunderstood expression "the invisible hand." Since the 2008 financial crisis, a growing body of critics of current economic thought and policy have called attention to these and other such flawed foundations and disciplinary biases. Thomas Piketty recalls that the origin of economics is the word *Oikonomia* from the Greek for household management and agriculture, which stems from the most intimate, collaborative form of human togetherness in the home. Calling attention to the specific language of economics, Tomáš Sedláček argues "modern economic theories based on rigorous modelling are nothing more than … metanarratives retold in different (mathematical?) language" (Sedláček 5). He goes on to emphasise that

> there is at least as much wisdom to be learned from our own philosophers, myths, religions, and poets as from exact and strict mathematical models of economic behaviour […] there is more religion, myth, and archetype in economics than there is mathematics. (9)

Whereas I have chosen Aesop's tale to illustrate the economic beliefs encoded in storytelling, Sedláček uses the 5,000-year old Sumerian epic *The Tale of Gilgamesh* and parables from the Bible, Old Testament and the Torah.

The above lineage demonstrates the centre of economics as concerned with human interaction, based on relationships and informed by
values, morals, and opinions, such as feelings of obligation, and gen-
erosity. If we understand the economy not in the narrow sense of finance
and market that dominates today, but in the broader sociological and anthropological sense of human economies, then the similarities with literary studies becomes clear: both disciplines model, interpret, analyse,
and critique the symbolic, cultural, social, and political expressions of
human exchange and interaction. Though the turn to mathematical for-
mulae, empirical and statistical data as the language of modern economics makes it hard for the discipline to see its underlying constructions,
the notion of "imagined economies," as John Clarke points out in the
first chapter of this collection, reopens space for critical consideration.
As Clarke also mentions, "imagined economies" also references Benedict Anderson's *Imagined Communities* (1983), which in turn nods in
the direction of Frankfurt School structuralists in order to deconstruct
the hegemonic common-sense reality that is, nevertheless, founded on
particular ideologies, perpetuated in governmental, educational and
other state apparatuses and promulgated by social and cultural mores.

Another commonality between imagined economies and Anderson's
imagined communities is the importance of the rise of the novel. Anderson, and later Timothy Brennan, in *Salman Rushdie and the Third
World: Myths of the Nation* (1989) and Edward Said, in *Culture and
Imperialism* (1993), argue that the nation and the novel are unimaginable
without each other. Literary economists similarly claim that the rise of
the novel coincides with the invention of modern economics, ensuring
thereby the normalisation of the new economic mode into the form of
cultural expression that came to dominate until eclipsed by visual media
in the late 20th century (Osteen and Woodmansee).[1]

---

1   What I do not mean by "imaginary" is either a Lacanian psychoanalysis aim-
    ing to separate out the symbolic and real, or an analysis of dystopian fantasy
    or science fiction, as suggested by Jameson ("Future City") on what he calls

By the time of the 2008 financial crisis, the range of textual formats engaging with the (un)believability of the global financial system had extended to include film, TV series, and documentaries, as well as an emerging form of popular, journalistic writing for a general readership by professors of economics themselves. When reviewers of Thomas Piketty's book tour of *Capital in the Twenty-First Century* dub the Parisian professor a "rock-star economist" (Tett 2014) and imagine a movie in which Piketty is played by Colin Firth (Moore 2014), and when the fictionalised documentary of the 2008 sub-prime collapse, *The Big Short* (2015), features actor Margot Robbie breaking the fourth wall to explain mortgage bonds to a captivated but bewildered audience, all sense of a split between "real" and "imagined" economics is rendered nonsensical.

Indeed, since the 2008 financial crisis, there has been an outpouring of film, TV series, documentaries, fiction and non-fiction about the economy.[2] Yet while all these media texts identify structural problems of global capitalism, and even though they often rigorously critique its inbuilt inequality and unfairness, they offer very few constructive alternatives: it is after all easier to criticise the system than to fully imagine its replacement. As George Monbiot sets out in the opening lines of *Out of the Wreckage: A New Politics for an Age of Crisis*:

"the attempt to imagine capitalism by way of imagining the end of the world."

2   Financial crisis fiction includes novels by well-known authors, including John Lanchester, Marina Lewycka, Lionel Shiver, C. K. Stead, and Sebastian Faulks. British film includes I, Daniel Blake (dir. Ken Loach, 2016) and Born Equal (dir. Dominic Savage, 2006); televised series include Billions (prod. Showtime, 2016) and Follow the Money (prod. Danmark Radio, 2016); documentary-style film includes The Wolf of Wall Street (dir. Martin Scorsese, 2013), The Big Short (dir. Adam McKay, 2015), Inequality for All (dir. Jacob Kornbluth, 2013), Capitalism: A Love Story (dir. Michael Moore, 2009).

[Y]ou cannot take away someone's story without giving them a new one. It is not enough to challenge an old narrative, however outdated and discredited it may be. Change happens only when you replace it with another. [...] Those who tell the stories run the world. (1)

Paraphrasing Frederic Jameson, it seems easier to imagine the end of the world than the end of capitalism (Jameson). The imagination required to think of alternative forms of socio-economic relations would appear to be in short supply.

Several critics diagnose a lack of imagination as the problem behind seeming paralysis to tackle pressing global issues such as runaway capitalism and its resultant impact on people and the environment (see Frase; Harvey; Mason). Anthropologist David Graeber, in his long-range 5,000-year history of the concept of debt, diagnoses today

[a] certain collapse of our collective imaginations. It's almost as if people had been led to believe that the era's technological advances and its greater overall social complexity ha[s] had the effect of *reducing* our political, social, and economic possibilities, rather than expanding them. Instead of unleashing visions, it ha[s] made visionary politics of any sort impossible. (393-94; italics in original)

Yet, if social scientists such as Graeber seem to be calling for more interdisciplinary help with figuring the imaginary, little input can be expected from the humanities, which are also suffering from stultification following 40 years of Margaret Thatcher's "there is no alternative" narrative that established neoliberalism in the late 1970s. In today's increasingly neoliberalising university, the humanities are under pressure to justify their value in economic terms, in which concepts of the imagination, critical thinking, 'soft' skills, literacy and foreign languages have little use-value. In the current late-capitalist, developed world that has almost fully succeeded in attributing financial values to formerly non-financialised things – including the commons, water, air, education, knowledge, and ideas – the humanities have been so sidelined, and literature so devalued,[3] that it is hard to even imagine that these disciplines might have an important role to play as interpreting or critiquing economic beliefs. Within this context of an apparent cultural, social, political and economic impasse arises the challenge for literature and economics to work together to figure and reconfigure our present and potential imagined economies.

Indications of fruitful collaboration appear in the increasing frequency of the word "narrative" in both specialist and mainstream discourse. The term refers most clearly to the domain of literary and cultural studies, but when applied to economics works to shift seemingly objective information into the realm of subjective interpretation, which opens space for ethical questions of the economy's role in human flourishing to emerge. To remember that the economy does not exist without people at its centre, who create and shape the economic narrative according to various, shifting, and plural belief systems, taps into the ethical and broader philosophical foundations of the discipline. Recasting the hitherto accepted facts of free-market globalisation rather as constructed narratives motivated by encouraged greed is a strategy for deconstructing the hegemony of mainstream political economy by turning truth into story. Examples of neoliberal tenets questioned or even discredited include: the supposed self-balancing mechanism of an unregulated financial market, the derailing of which caused the 2008 financial crisis; the belief in eternal growth that makes it impossible to respond to the planet's finite resources; the emphasis on human labour in the workplace as the highest social value at the same time as jobs are becoming more precarious and more automated; and the myths of the "rising tide lifts all boats" and of "trickle-down economics," used to support tax breaks and investment incentives for the super-rich yet debunked by evidence of growing wealth inequality. Deconstructing truths into their

---

3   In the US context, Morson and Schapiro claim: "In the late 1960s, nearly 18 percent of bachelor's degrees came from the humanities, but by 2010 this number had shrunk to 8 percent" (201).

driving narratives is even evident in the titles of popular economics books such as *Zombie Economics* (Quiggin), *Animal Spirits* (Akerlof and Shiller), *Kicking Away the Ladder* (Chang), and *The Great Divide* (Stiglitz).

Post-financial crisis, such popular economics texts aimed at a non-specialist reading public openly draw on literary imagery and cultural images in their challenges to the dominant narrative about how the economy works. Emphasis on the use of imagery in the above literature review suggests that thinking of economic alternatives has to start in the imaginary and upturn the reality we know and experience. Herein lies not only a space for new ways of thinking the form and function of the economy, but also offers a reinvigorated role for the humanities, particularly literary studies. Gary Saul Morson and Morton Schapiro, a literary scholar and an economist who teach and write together, are emphatic that literature, by foregrounding ethical and critical judgements, is crucial to fostering understanding of what the economy is for. In *Cents and Sensibility: What Economics Can Learn from the Humanities*, they make the audacious claim that literature should be brought to bear on governance, policy-making, and economic data: "[b]y using stories, we don't mean that they should be employed simply to illustrate the results of behavioural models, but instead that they be used to inform the creation of models themselves" (Morson and Schapiro 13). Their advocacy of interdisciplinary work that brings together humanities and social sciences offers one important model for imaginary economics.

While all the above attempts to view economics from a literary and cultural standpoint have been influential in my thinking for the present chapter, the exercise in interpreting and re-imagining "The Ant and the Grasshopper" is most directly inspired by Kate Raworth's recent *Doughnut Economics: Seven Ways to Think Like a 21st-Century Economist*. Raworth begins from the premise that the narrativity of economics is self-evident: "[e]verybody's saying it: we need a new economic story, a narrative of our shared economic future that is fit for the twenty-first century" (Raworth 12). Her text marks a departure from the common technique of popular economic texts that predominantly critique the economy in great detail, ending on a note of optimism in a final chapter that vaguely gestures towards solutions. Rather, Raworth's book from the beginning argues for constructive change. Her book may be part of a shift in popular economic writing from critique to creativity, as evidenced in the titles of other very recently published texts, including Peter Frase's *Four Futures: Life after Capitalism*, Paul Mason's *Postcapitalism: A Guide to Our Future*, Jeffrey Sachs's *Building the New American Economy: Smart, Fair, & Sustainable*, and Mary Robinson's *Climate Justice: Hope, Resilience, and the Fight for a Sustainable Future*. In thinking outside of current economic parameters, imagination necessarily comes to the fore, a point most clearly made by Raworth, who replaces the images that define 20th-century economics with new metaphors and visual images, including the doughnut of her book's title, that represent the sustainable, safe, just, and fair economic practices she advocates. Such change in economic criticism goes hand in hand with activism within university economics departments for curriculum change, notably the Rethinking Economics movement.[4]

To return, then, to economic readings of "The Ant and the Grasshopper," is an exercise in revealing the hidden biases and beliefs of our current neoliberal times. To heed the call from critical economists to question the foundations that at first seem self-evident opens up space to allow and encourage a questioning of the factual inevitability and ethical desirability of accepting the story as it first appears. Finally, by practicing the kind of imaginary economics that drives Raworth's call to rewrite the economic story fit for the 21st century, readers are invited to become co-writers to update and redraw "The Ant and the Grasshopper."

Aesop's fables are remarkable for having remained in public circulation, notably in ecclesiastical and educational circles, since their first

---

4   www.rethinkeconomics.org/; the German-speaking world association is the Network for Pluralist Economics: www.plurale-oekonomik.de/netzwerk-plurale-oekonomik/.

record in Greek literature and philosophy in the 5th century BC.[5] Today, Jean de la Fontaine's collected *Fables* (1668), which updated and modernised the stories in verse in the early-modern period, are perhaps the most well-known early examples of the craze for oral tales and fairy tales that were so instrumental in developing the "imagined community" (Anderson) of emergent nations. La Fontaine's "The Ant and the Grasshopper" introduces finance overtly to the tale: the grasshopper, or cicada in the French version, asks her "neighbour" ant for a loan:

> Asking for a loan of grist,
> A seed or two so she'd subsist
> Just until the coming spring.
> She said, "I'll pay you everything
> Before fall, my word as animal,
> Interest and principal." (Spector n.p.)

The ant, whose "finest virtue" is that she is "no hasty lender," refuses the loan, and the story ends on a note of moral superiority from the smug ant, which mocks the starving grasshopper with the final words, "you sang? […] / Now dance the winter away."

As all readings of history are necessarily informed by norms of the present, interpretations of Aesop stories starting from La Fontaine's versions are framed within the capitalist context of social relations: the perspective that enables publications to add the moral punchline to save now in order to have something to spend later. Although obviously no government is going to cite this – or any – story as an economic model, many policies are based on exactly this kind of moral judgement. In the United Kingdom, for example, the decline of the welfare state and criminalisation of poverty and unemployment by austerity politics send the message that welfare beneficiaries are useless grasshoppers partying

---

5   Analysis of pre-capitalist interpretations lies outside the scope of this paper, although certainly interpretations of Aesop's fables predate modern economics.

away their benefit money earned by hard-working, tax-paying ants. Within the national ant nest, the opportunistic grasshopper is easily construed as an immigrant, a foreign species towards which citizens are not expected to show any affinity or obligation. A Marxist reading, however, could invert the power relations to construe a different division of labour, one in which the ants are the exploited working-class overseen by a leisured class of singing grasshoppers living off inherited and invested wealth. In this reading, the grasshopper expects to be given food that it does not expect to work for. From this perspective, the ant's refusal may be seen as a triumph of the many over the few.

By contrast with the above meritocratic or even Darwinian reading that rewards self-sufficiency and hard work, the fable can also stimulate empathy for the outcast grasshopper, calling on readers' social values of shared responsibility to protect life and well-being. The influence of 20ᵗʰ-century socialist and welfare-state values, as well as the modern turn away from violence and unhappy endings in children's stories, are also evident in adaptations of the fable. In both, Walt Disney's 1934 animated version and Leo Lionni's popular children's book *Frederick* (1967), the workers share their provisions with the artist.[6] Although these stories overtly claim that culture, music, and art are also valued in society, the covert construction of the grasshopper figure as the weaker member of society – Disney's grasshopper catches a bad cold and Lionni's distracted daydreamer needs constant help from the others – represents an unequal dynamic based on benevolence and charity. Disney's grasshopper is even successfully re-educated of its work ethic. Having begun the story singing "the world owes me a living," the grasshopper thanks the ants for their hospitality by performing a song for them, "I owe the world a living" (Baxter).

---

6 Lionni's version features one community of mice rather than the usual two groups of ants and grasshopper. Here, Frederick is a dreamer that appreciates the beauty of nature and poetry all summer. When winter comes and the mice have eaten all their supplies, Frederick keeps them entertained with beautiful stories of nature.

Regardless of one's reading, all the above versions of the fable result in uncomfortable reading experiences, without clear resolutions or happy endings. Within a competitive model of life as a Darwinian struggle in which there will be winners and losers, the rational individual man, *homo economicus*, would conclude that the grasshopper is doomed to die out. Indeed, the real-world analogue of mass extinction of animals – particularly insects – brought about by human destruction of habitat exactly for the increased production of human supplies, suggests the truth of Aesop's ancient fable. Within the neoliberal primacy of the market at the expense of the state, household and commons, the hope contained within the story, that the grasshopper's cultural labour can be traded for the ant's productive labour, is largely foreclosed. Since the drawback of the state under neoliberalism, culture, arts and music have suffered drastic funding cuts, are today almost absent in schools (Jeffreys), and as argued above, increasingly squeezed out of academia.

As a narrative with a 2,500-year history of rewriting, however, we do not have to accept "The Ant and the Grasshopper" as a classical economics story of competition and natural attrition. To envisage a scenario with an ethical and sustainable outcome, in which both the ant and the grasshopper can survive and thrive, requires thinking anew our relationships with other people, other species, and nature. Contextualising and thus interpreting Aesop's fable is an exercise in using the imaginary to rethink economics. Following Monbiot's call to replace the dominant story and Raworth's bid to write the economic narratives fit for the 21st century, we can rewire Aesop's fable to fit alternative values. In the same vein as critical economists' exposure of falsehoods and myths tenaciously embedded in mainstream economics, Aesop's limited knowledge of insect ecology requires correcting.

Like much about classical economics, a capitalist interpretation of Aesop's fable, such as those above, contain glaring ignorance of the non-market aspects of the economy that, having no direct financial value, are often absent from economic models: namely the commons, the social reproduction of unpaid household labour, and the state. Certainly, the insects' ecological niches are not paid and their motivations are not financial. Rather, the ant and the grasshopper meet in spaces which Karl Polanyi called the "embedded" economy, here in the commons while taking care of social reproduction in participating in and providing for their respective communities. Anthropomorphising the insects as individual rational economic man further fails on other accounts – not least because the 'worker' ants that forage for food are female. In nature, an adult grasshopper does not live more than a few weeks and its larvae overwinter underground. Thus, it is neither going to steal from the ant (assuming that they even shared an ecological niche) nor die of hunger.

For the ant's part, as synergistic superorganisms, that which the Greeks called *Eusocial* ('good' social), like bees and coral, ants do not collect food for themselves but for the colony. Aesop's female worker ant will spend part of her adult life gathering food and feeding larvae, and in winter she will hibernate in the colony to collectively keep it warm. Most ant species do not store any food in their nests, so there is no hoarding for winter as Aesop imagined.[7] Indeed, the idea that one individual works only for its own future, as encoded in the dialogue between one ant and one grasshopper, is anathema to both species. In this light, the insects' social worlds offer prosocial models that humans might take heed of. Indeed, the current push towards sustainable futures

---

7   As the focus of this paper is interpretative and literary rather than factual and entomological, facts about insects were sourced online, including from National Geographic's Photo Ark project, Pest World for Kids, and relevant Wikipedia pages. While I recognise the flaws and biases of such unsubstantiated, popular knowledge sources, particularly Wikipedia collaborative writing, the availability today of non-expert, non-academic information is important to my project's aim to break down academic and disciplinary boundaries. Both economics and English suffer from an elitist reputation as being "too hard" for non-experts to approach and engage with (see Kennedy). On the contrary, imagining alternative economies requires an immense effort in collective, collaborative thinking open to the public.

geared not to instant consumer gratification but rather the stewardship of the earth for future generations work in this direction.

Instead of anthropomorphising the ant and grasshopper, with its implied anthropogenic centring of humans in the web of life, a better approach might be to zoomorphise the humans. We might find inspiration by thinking of humans more as insects, as interconnected to a huge intergenerational community of which we only ever see one small part, working not only for each other now, but participating in building a home for future generations we will never live to see. We might also do well to remember that grasshoppers (along with cicadas, crickets, and cockroaches) are some of the oldest creatures on earth: predating the dinosaurs, it is likely they will outlive us as well. Such deep-time thinking underpins the current shift even in economics to strive for sustainable ecological balances for the safety of future generations. Precepts of the circular economy, such as those expounded in *Doughnut Economics*, similarly reject unnatural expectations of indefinite economic growth in favour of regenerative, distributive and dynamic circular flows owned and controlled not by *homo economicus* but by the entire community network.

To illustrate the kind of thinking needed to imagine such different ways of imagining economics, Raworth draws, as this chapter does, from imagery inspired by nature. She argues for a change in understanding economics away from images of the masculine, the mechanical and the linear.[8] Instead she posits visual and metaphorical images of the feminine,[9] of nature, and of circularity. For example, she reconsiders system

---

8   Raworth's examples include: the figure of rational economic man and the dominance of men throughout the history of economic thought; Paul Samuelson's Circular Flow Diagram; and linear graphs representing theories of GDP growth, supply-demand equilibrium, and Kuznets's inequality bell-curve.

9   By feminine, I mean Raworth's emphasis throughout her book on feminist economics (and economists) and her insistence on the centrality of the "core" economy (78) of the household and the commons to all human well-being.

theory within an extended metaphor of gardening (127, 156), and re-places boom-and-bust dynamics with an equilibrium model wittily rep-resented by the chicken-and-egg (139-40). Her model is rooted firmly in a particular sense of ethics that recalls the moral philosophy at the root of early modern economics. Raworth imagines an economist's version of the Greek Hippocratic Oath taken by doctors to "minimise the risk of harm – especially to the most vulnerable – in the face of uncertainty," and "work with humility, by making transparent the assumptions and shortcomings of your models, and by recognising alternative economic perspectives and tools" (161). Reading Aesop's fable through these and other such sustainable and ethical frameworks rejects the inequality cre-ated by competition in which the ant wins in resource allocation, to in-stead foster and maintain an oscillating equilibrium with reinforcing and balancing feedback loops in which both ant and grasshopper fill their respective ecological niches.

To consider the story *not* as thinly disguised allegories of human character encourages readers to marvel at the insects' unique abilities, such as the elaborate mating rituals that produce the grasshopper's "mu-sic," and ants' ability to carry huge loads and communicate via their complex hive minds. To accept that growth also entails degrowth, and that generation engenders both re- and degeneration, allows the reader to accept the natural end of the grasshopper's life-cycle, having safely laid its eggs to hatch in spring, and the ant's labour for the complex so-cial structure and architecture of its city-like colony. Finally, to read

---

The book outlines various economic aspects of gender inequality, including the relative absence of female economists in the history of the discipline, and the gendered nature of unpaid labour, the care economy, and social repro-duction. Her focus, however, is not to critique the marginalisation of women or suggest gender roles or stereotypes, but rather to introduce her general readership to central aspects required for an economy focused on human well-being, flourishing nature and planetary balance.

"with humility" means resisting making the kind of final moral judgement often printed in modern editions of Aesop Fables, in recognition
of the plurality of perspectives brought to this ancient tale.

This chapter has argued for imaginary economics as a mechanism
through which to recognise the changing disciplines of both literary
studies and economics. At the same time as "narrative" has become a
buzz-word across disciplines and in media and journalism, there has
been a concomitant call from across the social sciences to remember
both the philosophical roots of economics and the historical importance
of literary and cultural studies in shaping social, political and economic
formations. The exercise of rereading and rewriting "The Ant and the
Grasshopper" taps into these trends to illuminate the common references
of shared narratives through which we each make sense of the world, a
reminder that we can all contribute to activating the imagination and
promoting – indeed creating – a robust economic imaginary that is ethi-
cally and sustainably fit for the 21st century.

REFERENCES

Akerlof, George, and Robert Shiller. *Animal Spirits: How Human Psy-
chology Drives the Economy and Why It Matters for Global Capitalism.* Princeton University Press, 2009.

Anderson, Benedict. *Imagined Communities: Reflections on the Origin
and Spread of Nationalism.* Verso, 1991.

Baxter, Devon. "Disney's "The Grasshopper And The Ants" (1934)."
Cartoon Research, 23 November 2016, cartoonresearch.com/index.
php/disneys-the-grasshopper-and-the-ants-1934/.

Brennan, Timothy. *Salman Rushdie and the Third World: Myths of the
Nation.* Palgrave Macmillan, 1989.

Chang, Ha-Joon. *Kicking Away the Ladder: Development Strategy in
Historical Perspective.* Anthem, 2003.

Frase, Peter. *Four Futures: Life after Capitalism.* Verso, 2016.

Graeber, David. *Debt: The First 5,000 Years.* 2011. Melville, 2014.

Harvey, David. *Spaces of Hope*. California University Press, 2000.

Jameson, Frederic. "Future City." *New Left Review*, 21 May-June 2003, pp. 65-79.

Jeffreys, Branwen. "Creative Subjects Being Squeezed, Schools Tell BBC." 30 January 2018, www.bbc.com/news/education-42862996.

Kennedy, Melissa. "Reading Like Economists to Reimagine the Humanities." *Studia Neophilologica*, vol. 91, no. 2, forthcoming 2019.

Lionni, Leo. *Frederick*. 1967. Knopf, 1995.

Mason, Paul. *Postcapitalism: A Guide to Our Future*. Allen Lane, 2015.

Monbiot, George. *Out of the Wreckage: A New Politics for an Age of Crisis*. Verso, 2017.

Moore, Heidi. "Thomas Piketty is a Rock-Star Economist – Can He Rewrite the American Dream?" *The Guardian*, 27 April 2014, www.theguardian.com/commentisfree/2014/apr/27/thomas-piketty-economist-american-dream.

Morson, Gary Saul, and Morton Schapiro. *Cents and Sensibility: What Economics Can Learn from the Humanities*. Princeton University Press, 2017.

Osteen, Mark, and Martha Woodmansee, editors. *The New Economic Criticism: Studies at the Intersection of Literature and Economics*. Routledge, 1999.

Piketty, Thomas. *Capital in the Twenty-First Century*. 2013. Translated by Arthur Goldhammer, Belknap, 2014.

Quiggin, John. *Zombie Economics: How Dead Ideas Still Walk Among Us*. Princeton University Press, 2012.

Raworth. Kate. *Doughnut Economics: Seven Ways to Think Like a 21st-Century Economist*. Random House, 2017.

Robinson, Mary. *Climate Justice: Hope, Resilience, and the Fight for a Sustainable Future*. Bloomsbury, 2018.

Sachs, Jeffrey. *Building the New American Economy: Smart, Fair, & Sustainable*. Columbia University Press, 2017.

Said, Edward. *Culture and Imperialism*. Vintage, 1993.

Sedláček, Tomáš. *Economics of Good and Evil: The Quest for Economic Meaning from Gilgamesh to Wall Street.* Oxford University Press, 2011.

Spector, Norman B., editor. *The Complete Fables of Jean de la Fontaine.* Northwestern University Press, 2019, lafontaine.mmlc.northwestern.edu/fables/cigale_fourmi_en.html.

Stiglitz, Joseph. *The Great Divide: Unequal Societies and What We Can Do About Them.* Norton, 2015.

Tett, Gillian. "Lessons from a Rock-Star Economist." *Financial Times,* 24 April 2014, www.ft.com/content/0421d04e-cb42-11e3-ba95-001 44feabdc0.

Authors

Jason Grant Allen read law in Australia, Germany, the United States, and the United Kingdom. Currently a Senior Fellow at the Weizenbaum Institute for the Networked Society, Jason holds a research position at the Centre for British Studies, Humboldt-Universität zu Berlin, and affiliations at UTAS, UNSW, QMUL CCLS and the Cambridge Centre for Alternative Finance. His work explores the interface of legal theory, social ontology, heterodox economics, and technology. He is presently engaged in two research projects that explore the legal and economic aspects of money, with particular emphasis on communication between German and Anglophone theory in the 20th century and the way that technology problematises received legal categories.

Rebecca Bramall is a Senior Lecturer in Media and Communications at London College of Communication, University of the Arts London. Rebecca's research explores the relationship between culture and economy, with a current focus on taxation imaginaries. Key publications include *The Cultural Politics of Austerity: Past and Present in Austere Times* (Palgrave Macmillan, 2013) and a special issue of *New Formations* on Austerity (2016).

Olivier Butzbach is a researcher in Economics at the University of Campania "Luigi Vanvitelli" (Italy). His work is interdisciplinary and focuses on long- and medium-term transformations of not-for-profit banks in Europe, applying concepts and methods from economics and sociology to the historical emergence, development and decline of alternative organizational forms in the financial industry.

John Clarke is an Emeritus Professor at the UK's Open University and a recurrent Visiting Professor at Central European University. He is currently working on the turbulent times marked by the rise of nationalist, populist and authoritarian politics. Recent publications include *Making Policy Move: Towards a politics of translation and assemblage* (with Dave Bainton, Noémi Lendvai and Paul Stubbs; Policy Press, 2015) and *Critical Dialogues: Thinking Together in Turbulent Times*, based on a series of conversations with people who have helped him to think (Policy Press, 2019).

Christiane Eisenberg is a historian and Professor of British History and Society at the Centre for British Studies, Humboldt Universität zu Berlin. Her current field of work is the history of the market economy and commercial culture in Britain. She is currently writing a book on the "Sporting Spirit of Capitalism", which deals with 18th-century Britain's departure into the modern economy.

Jessica Fischer is a researcher in Literary and Cultural Studies. Her doctoral thesis entitled *Agency. The Entrepreneurial Self in Narratives of Transformation* explores neoliberal discourses in contemporary British fiction. Currently, she is investigating adventure stories for a postdoc project with the working title "ADVENTURE. British Stories and Visuals of Venturing Subjects at the Turn of the 20th Century". *Imagined Economies* is based on the lecture series which she organised for Humboldt-Universität zu Berlin in summer 2018.

Jana Gohrisch teaches British literatures and cultures at the University of Hannover (Germany) and has a special interest in postcolonial literatures in English, especially black British and Caribbean, West and South African. She is currently working on post-emancipation constructions of agency in fictional and non-fictional texts about the British West Indies since the mid-19th century.

Melissa Kennedy is Professor of English Culture and Literature at the Pädagogische Hochschule Oberösterreich and Privatdozentin at the University of Vienna. She has extensively published in the field of literary economics, including a monograph *Narratives of Inequality: Postcolonial Literary Economics* (Palgrave, 2017) and a co-edited special issue of *Interventions*, "All that Glitters Is Not Gold: Pacific Critiques of Globalization" (vol. 19, no. 7, 2017). Her current research works with the concept of imaginary economics to analyse literary and cultural representations of a fair, just, sustainable and collaborative life-world.

Luke Martell is a Teaching Fellow and Professor in Sociology, University of Sussex, with research interests in socialism, social alternatives, social democracy, globalisation and social movements.

Gesa Stedman is professor of British Culture and Literature at the Centre for British Studies, Humboldt-Universität zu Berlin. Her main interests range from early-modern cultural exchange to Victorian discourses on emotion, contemporary literature, literary sociology, cultural studies, gender history, and most recently, Anglophone writing on Berlin.

Cultural Studies

Elisa Ganivet
Border Wall Aesthetics
Artworks in Border Spaces

2019, 250 p., hardcover, ill.
79,99 € (DE), 978-3-8376-4777-8
E-Book: 79,99 € (DE), ISBN 978-3-8394-4777-2

Jocelyne Porcher, Jean Estebanez (eds.)
Animal Labor
A New Perspective on Human-Animal Relations

2019, 182 p., hardcover
99,99 € (DE), 978-3-8376-4364-0
E-Book: 99,99 € (DE), ISBN 978-3-8394-4364-4

Andreas Sudmann (ed.)
The Democratization of Artificial Intelligence
Net Politics in the Era of Learning Algorithms

2019, 334 p., pb., col. ill.
49,99 € (DE), 978-3-8376-4719-8
E-Book: 49,99 € (DE), ISBN 978-3-8394-4719-2

**All print, e-book and open access versions of the titles in our list
are available in our online shop www.transcript-verlag.de/en!**

Cultural Studies

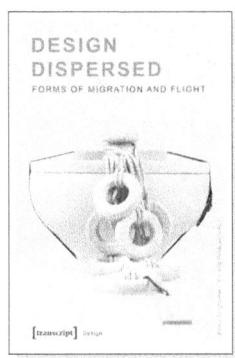

Burcu Dogramaci, Kerstin Pinther (eds.)
Design Dispersed
Forms of Migration and Flight

2019, 274 p., pb., col. ill.
34,99 € (DE), 978-3-8376-4705-1
E-Book: 34,99 € (DE), ISBN 978-3-8394-4705-5

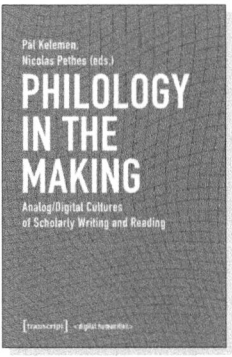

Pál Kelemen, Nicolas Pethes (eds.)
Philology in the Making
Analog/Digital Cultures of Scholarly Writing and Reading

2019, 316 p., pb., ill.
34,99 € (DE), 978-3-8376-4770-9
E-Book: 34,99 € (DE), ISBN 978-3-8394-4770-3

Chris Goldie, Darcy White (eds.)
Northern Light
Landscape, Photography and Evocations of the North

2018, 174 p., hardcover, ill.
79,99 € (DE), 978-3-8376-3975-9
E-Book: 79,99 € (DE), ISBN 978-3-8394-3975-3

**All print, e-book and open access versions of the titles in our list
are available in our online shop www.transcript-verlag.de/en!**

GPSR Authorized Representative: Easy Access System Europe, Mustamäe tee 50, 10621 Tallinn, Estonia, gpsr.requests@easproject.com

www.ingramcontent.com/pod-product-compliance
Lightning Source LLC
Chambersburg PA
CBHW061755120626

46550CB00005B/2001